THE SOUL OF A CEO

*Rebuilding from Collapse to Clarity,
One Truth at a Time*

CHRISTOPHER AMATO

COPYRIGHT © 2025 AMATO INTERNATIONAL LLC.
ALL RIGHTS RESERVED.

AUTHOR: CHRISTOPHER AMATO

ISBN (PAPERBACK): 979-8-9940228-0-1

NO PART OF THIS PUBLICATION MAY BE REPRODUCED, DISTRIBUTED, OR TRANSMITTED IN ANY FORM OR BY ANY MEANS, INCLUDING PHOTOCOPYING, RECORDING, OR OTHER ELECTRONIC OR MECHANICAL METHODS, WITHOUT PRIOR WRITTEN PERMISSION OF THE PUBLISHER, EXCEPT IN THE CASE OF BRIEF QUOTATIONS EMBODIED IN CRITICAL REVIEWS AND PERMITTED NONCOMMERCIAL USES UNDER COPYRIGHT LAW.

PUBLISHED BY AMATO INTERNATIONAL LLC - SCOTTSDALE, ARIZONA

COVER DIRECTION & DESIGN: JEREMIE KING & ANDREA KING JCT42.COM
INTERIOR DESIGN, LAYOUT, & DEVELOPMENTAL EDITING: ANDREA KING / JUNCTION 42 STUDIO

PRINTED IN THE UNITED STATES OF AMERICA.

DISCLAIMER

THIS BOOK IS INTENDED FOR INFORMATIONAL AND EDUCATIONAL PURPOSES ONLY. IT REFLECTS THE AUTHOR'S PERSONAL EXPERIENCES, PERSPECTIVES, AND INTERPRETATIONS OF LEADERSHIP, MINDSET, EMOTIONAL WELL-BEING, AND PERSONAL GROWTH.

IT IS **NOT** A SUBSTITUTE FOR PROFESSIONAL, PSYCHOLOGICAL, MEDICAL, LEGAL, FINANCIAL, OR BUSINESS ADVICE. READERS SHOULD CONSULT QUALIFIED PROFESSIONALS REGARDING ANY CONDITION, DECISION, OR CIRCUMSTANCE THAT REQUIRES SUCH EXPERTISE. THE AUTHOR AND PUBLISHER DISCLAIM ANY LIABILITY ARISING FROM THE USE OR MISUSE OF THE INFORMATION CONTAINED IN THIS BOOK.

EVERY READER'S SITUATION IS UNIQUE. USE DISCERNMENT, APPLY WHAT RESONATES, AND SEEK PROFESSIONAL GUIDANCE WHEN APPROPRIATE.

First Edition, 2025

DEDICATION

To the CEOs, entrepreneurs, and doers of this world. To the men and women who built lives through discipline and drive, yet somewhere along the way lost sight of who they really are.

If you've forgotten your identity, your worth, or the truth of what you carry, consider this your reminder.

You are worth the work. Rediscover yourself. Take the energy you've poured into everyone and everything else and direct it inward. Not as indulgence, but as responsibility. The world needs the version of you that is grounded, clear, and whole.

This journey isn't only for you. It's for the people who will benefit from you showing up as your truest self. I believe in that version. If I found my way back, you can too. And if enough of us do that, we make the world better, one honest leader at a time.

LIFE WILL WORK OUT PERFECTLY
- ALL THE RIGHT THINGS ARE ~~GOING TO HAPPEN~~ HAPPENING
- ALL THE RIGHT PEOPLE ~~WILL~~ COME TO ME
- ALL THE WRONG PEOPLE ~~WILL~~ LEAVE
- I ~~WILL~~ HAVE A BEAUTIFUL PEACEFUL HOME
- I ~~WILL~~ HAVE A DYNAMIC CAREER THAT GIVE ME PURPOSE
- I WILL WAKE UP NEXT TO THE LOVE OF MY LIFE
- I WILL HAVE DIVINE CONNECTION
- MY ART ~~WILL BE~~ IS IMPACTFUL
- I ~~WILL BE~~ AM RECOGNIZED FOR MY DEVOTION
- I CONTINUE TO TRAVEL THE WORLD AND MEET INCREDIBLE PEOPLE
- I ~~WILL BE~~ AM SEEN FOR WHO I AM
- I ~~WILL BE~~ AM APPRECIATED FOR ALL I

CONTENTS

Prologue: The Collapse — ix

Introduction: Why This Book Exists — xi

Part One: Power Without Soul

1. Not My Roller Coaster to Ride — 1
2. Rebuilding an Empire — 23
3. The Betrayal — 37

Part Two: The Descent

4. When the Empire Crumbles — 51
5. The Journey Down — 61
6. Facing The Darkness — 73

Part Three: The Rebuild

7. The Winding Road to Wholeness — 87
8. Forgiving Myself for Causing Pain — 97
9. Leadership Transformed by Energy — 109

Part Four: The Soul of Leadership

10. Rising from the Ashes — 123
11. The CEO as an Example of Healing — 139
12. Legacy Beyond Wealth — 149

Manifesto: The Soul of a CEO — 161
A Letter to My Younger Self — 163
About The Author — 165

PROLOGUE

The Collapse

From the outside, everything looked strong. The empire was intact. Revenue was up. The calendar was full, the inbox overflowing. People admired the grind, the constant movement, the picture of productivity.

But on the inside, cracks had already formed.

What no one tells you is that success can collapse under its own weight.

Busy does not equal effective.
Productivity does not equal progress.

You can build the tallest tower and still feel hollow inside. The meetings, the calls, the deals, all of it was scaffolding around a structure rotting at the core.

I thought that if I kept moving faster, the feeling would go away. That if I achieved more, the gnawing emptiness would be filled. But busyness is a false god. It demands everything and gives nothing.

The truth is simple: energy leaks equal burnout.

Every moment I spent chasing external validation, another client, another accolade, another nod of approval, was energy slipping through holes I refused to patch.

I leaked energy by saying yes when I should have said no.

By carrying what wasn't mine. By playing roles to please others. By fixing what was never broken in the first place.

It worked for a while. Until it didn't.

When the empire crumbled, it didn't fall in one dramatic crash. It decayed slowly, the way a rope frays until one final strand snaps.

Suddenly, I was no longer the leader in command of a thriving enterprise. I was a man running on fumes, scattered, and disconnected from myself.

That collapse, painful as it was, became the invitation. The moment I could no longer avoid the truth:

Success without soul is a hollow victory

INTRODUCTION

Why This Book Exists

For most of my life, I believed that being connected meant being included. To be at the table. To show up at every meeting, every event. To maintain the appearance that I belonged. If I was seen, I was valuable. If I stayed busy, I was safe.

And on the outside, it worked. My calendar was full. My inbox overflowed. Meetings stacked on top of meetings. I was producing, delivering, performing. People looked at my schedule and assumed it meant success.

But on the inside, cracks had formed.

Alan Watts once said that the ego's attempt to always be right is a defense mechanism. I lived that. I wore the mask of certainty, always seeking to prove my worth, always needing to be included, always defending my place.

It turns out that masks are heavy, and I was suffocating underneath my smile.

The collapse wasn't a single dramatic moment. It was the slow erosion of energy. The constant grind. The pressure to always be "on." The weight of carrying everyone else's needs and expectations.

Eventually, I found myself burned out, sitting in silence, staring at a calendar so full there was no space left for me.

That was the breaking point.

The turning point came when I started to shift my priorities inward. Instead of chasing validation, I began learning to look in the mirror and sit with what I saw. Not just the polished version, all of me. The past, the failures, the pain.

I began forgiving. Forgiving those who hurt me. Forgiving those who let me down. Most importantly, forgiving myself. In that forgiveness, I found power returning that I had unknowingly given away.

And with that power came a revelation:

IT'S NOT MY ROLLER COASTER TO RIDE

More on that in Chapter 1. This book exists because I know I'm not alone. Outward success doesn't protect anyone from inward collapse.

CEOs are people too.

I burned myself out chasing validation, spreading my energy too thin, and dumping my energy in the wrong places. I learned from that, and I'm writing this book to share that there's a different way.

This is not a book about tactics, hacks, or shortcuts. It's a book about soul. It's about healing what's within so that what you create and build actually lasts. It's about leading differently, with energy, with discipline, and with soul.

Many strong leaders have been through their own version of hell. They didn't stay stuck in it, they kept going through it, burned away the masks and lies and became whole.

My hope is that in sharing the path that nearly destroyed me it might free others from falling into the same holes I did.

The lessons I've learned aren't just for CEOs, they're for anyone ready to rise from the ashes of collapse and lead with authentic truth and soul.

If you're lucky enough to be reading this early in your journey, my hope is that you decide what yours looks like and begin to create it. If your journey is farther along and you have found yourself questioning your identity, my hope is that you remember your true self. You are worth it!

Author's Note:

If you're reading this, you've probably had a moment where everything fell apart, maybe quietly, maybe all at once. I know that moment.

It stripped away everything I thought defined me and forced me to see who I really was underneath the noise.

This book came from the wreckage, the lessons, and the slow process of finding peace after chasing everything else.

I've changed the names and details of others in this story, but what remains is real. The mistakes are mine. The awareness is mine. The growth is mine.

The people in these pages aren't villains or saviors. They're mirrors. Each one reflected something I needed to see, the parts I loved, the parts I denied, and the parts I had to finally face.

Without them, none of this healing would have been possible. I'm still in it as long as I'm alive.

Still learning. Still rebuilding. Sharing it here feels like the only honest thing to do.

You'll find this story at the beginning of each chapter, written in italics, for those who want to feel the full experience behind the principles.

PART ONE

POWER WITHOUT SOUL

CHAPTER 1

Not My Roller Coaster To Ride

"Your time is limited, so don't waste it living someone else's life."

Steve Jobs

I never intended to own a manufacturing company.

That was never the plan.

I wasn't chasing a dream of stainless tanks, forklifts, and the smell of solvents. I wanted a life built on strategy and movement, not machinery.

It started at a simple networking event, one of those meetings where most people exchange cards and half-listen to elevator pitches. I was talking with an insurance contact about a project we were collaborating on when a man walked in who had just come from his sister's funeral.

He looked tired in a way I recognized.

The kind of tiredness that sits behind your eyes when life has changed faster than you can catch up.

His sister, Mary, had owned a small manufacturing company. She had built it with her partner, Thomas, years earlier. After she passed, there was no succession plan, no transition, no one ready to take the wheel.

Her daughter Michelle was only eighteen. Bright, creative, and completely uninterested in running a factory. Thomas had retired but remained connected as the executor of her estate.

He was trying to keep things afloat long enough to protect the daughter's inheritance. The company itself wasn't part of that safety net; it was simply there, half-alive, drifting.

I listened as he described the situation. Something in me wanted to help. Not out of ambition, out of curiosity.

I told him I could fly to California, take a look, and see if the business had any chance of survival. Maybe it needed to close, maybe it needed to sell. I had no expectations, just a willingness to see clearly what was there.

When I walked through that facility for the first time, I could feel the energy of what had once been.

Machines stood quiet. Employees floated through their days the best they could without direction. The ledgers were chaos, invoices stacked on desks, it was incredible how fast it was unraveling.

Somehow, underneath the exhaustion, there was something solid. The formulas were good, the equipment capable, the customers loyal. The company wasn't dead, it was in limbo. It needed care and leadership.

It needed someone to believe in it again.

I went home and ran the analysis. The numbers told a hard story, but not a hopeless one. I saw a clear path forward if someone had the nerve to take it.

I found an investor named Walter, a man I respected and had worked with before. He was semi-retired and looking for a project to keep him active.

We agreed that he would fund the purchase, I would take twenty percent for putting the deal together, and we would rebuild side by side.

It felt like a clean plan.

Chase Bank held the company's line of credit, and every piece of equipment on the floor was collateralized against it. If the note wasn't paid, the bank would seize the assets and end the story overnight.

We scheduled the closing, prepared to pay the note, and set a meeting with the bank. Three days before that meeting, Walter backed out.

He told me it was more work than he wanted at this stage of life. I understood, but it left me staring at a deadline that could destroy everything before it began.

The employees had been told help was coming. The bank was waiting. I had seventy-two hours to find another way.

I didn't panic. I moved.

I called everyone in my network until I reached Steven, a quiet investor with two grown sons who often partnered with him on business ventures. I laid out the opportunity, the numbers, the urgency, and the potential upside if the company could be turned around.

Within three days we were on a plane to California.

We met with the bank, wired the payoff, and added a small injection of working capital to keep production alive. That was the moment ownership shifted. I was not to be a minority partner but the majority owner, President and CEO.

The title had my name on it now, and so did the responsibility.

I told myself I was saving a business. In reality, I had climbed into a roller coaster I didn't build, convinced I could steer it once the ride began. Time would tell.

Christopher Amato

The Lesson: The Ride Costs Energy

The roller coaster pulls up every day. Different paint job, same track.

A customer meltdown. A partner's crisis. A family emergency. Each one is an invitation to trade clarity for adrenaline.

That's the choice.
Do you get in, or do you stay grounded?

For years I thought riding the emotional ride was part of being a CEO, a father, a husband, a human.

Feel the highs when everything clicks. Feel the lows when everything crashes.

The truth is simpler: the ride costs energy, and energy is currency. When you spend it on things that aren't yours to carry, you deplete the reserves you need to lead.

The Temptation of the Ride

What do you do when something shows up that tempts you to jump into a car you don't need to be in?

It could be a customer upset about an order, an employee working through personal issues, or a business partner caught in conflict.

The natural instinct is to engage, to solve, to jump on the ride and get pulled into every twist and turn.

But here's the truth:

> ***Engaging emotionally in every situation doesn't make you stronger. It makes you drained.***

Boundaries don't mean you stop caring. They mean you care enough to stay steady, so you can lead with clarity when it's actually needed.

I've learned the hard way that scattered energy equals scattered direction. There was a time when I was trying to be everywhere at once, fixing client issues, coaching employees through personal struggles, keeping up appearances in my community.

> ***Urgency is often an emotion in a costume. Pause before you answer.***

I told myself I was being responsible, being a good leader, being available. In reality, I was burning energy on rides that weren't mine. When it came time to make real decisions for my business, I didn't have the clarity or the capacity left.

Mini Practice: The next time a problem shows up, pause and ask: Is this my roller coaster to ride? Notice what changes when you choose not to get in.

The Highs Can Derail You

The roller coaster isn't just negative. Sometimes the high is just as destabilizing. I remember being in Roatán, standing on the edge of paradise, opportunities left and right.

The rush was intoxicating.

The anticipation was like climbing the first hill on a coaster. You can see the drop coming and the adrenaline kicks in.

Here's the catch: even the high can drain you if it's your only fuel.

When motivation fades, discipline carries you. Staying steady matters just as much when everything's going great as when it all feels like it's falling apart.

Discipline is freedom. The habits you resist are the ones that set you free. Early in my career, I fought structure because I thought freedom meant doing whatever I wanted. I learned quickly that without discipline, I was at the mercy of circumstance. Discipline built rhythm. Rhythm created momentum. And momentum eventually created mastery.

Reflection in Action: Think about the last time you hit a win. Did you stay on track, or did the high pull you into overconfidence or distraction?

Business Boundaries

As a CEO, I've watched business partners go through divorces, employees wrestle with challenges, customers lash out under stress. Each one is another roller coaster pulling up. If you ride every single one, your capacity collapses. You can't lead if your energy is scattered.

> ***Energy is currency.***
> ***Humans have a finite balance.***

Every ride you take that isn't yours to ride burns through that balance. When the balance is gone, you've got nothing left for the things only you can handle.

I once had a supplier meltdown that could've easily hijacked my week. Phone calls, emails, finger pointing. Chaos spreads fast when one link in the chain breaks. I caught myself getting pulled into every detail. Then I stopped and asked: What's actually mine here? My role was to make the next clear decision, not to carry the emotional storm of every vendor. That one pause kept me from riding a ride that wasn't mine.

Exercise to Build Clarity: For one week, write down every situation that tries to pull you in. At the end of the week, circle which ones were actually yours. Most won't be. That's your proof of where your boundaries need to tighten.

Energy as Currency

Energy spent is energy invested. Whether it's positive or negative, there's always an ROI. The problem is most leaders don't realize they're spending on cheap junk.

They waste energy chasing external validation, over-explaining themselves, or playing roles to please everyone.

It's like throwing cash at slot machines and being surprised when nothing comes back.

I've done it. I've said yes when I should've said no.

I've played mediator when no one asked me to.

I've explained myself five different ways to people who weren't listening in the first place.

Every time, I walked away drained, wondering why my focus was shot for the rest of the day.

Focused energy, on the other hand, compounds. When I put energy into systems, strategy, or relationships that actually mattered, the return was exponential. That's the ROI of energy.

Spend it on cheap junk, get cheap results. Spend it aligned, get exponential results.

Practical Move: Write down three recurring energy leaks. For each one, draft a single boundary sentence you can use next time it shows up. Example: "I care about you, and I'm not taking on your ride."

Staying Even Keel

There's nothing wrong with emotion. The problem is being controlled by it. High or low, if adrenaline is driving the car, you're not making centered decisions.

Stepping back doesn't make you cold. It keeps you clear.

Your nervous system sets the tone.

I walked into rooms where the tension was thick, and without saying a word, my calm shifted the space.

The opposite is true too.

When I walked in scattered, the whole room picked up on it.

That's the reality of leadership: people feel you before they hear you.

So. Become the calm.

In the eye of the storm comes clarity. When your nervous system is regulated, your energy commands.

That energy changes situations, relationships, and outcomes.

It's not a theory, it's observable reality.

You can care deeply without absorbing chaos. Think umbrella, not sponge.

Quick Anchor: Create a daily practice that reminds you you're steady. Whether it's a morning walk, five minutes of breathing, or writing down the three priorities only you can do that day.

Subtraction as Progress

The new definition of progress isn't addition, it's subtraction. Subtracting distractions, obligations, and the need to prove yourself creates space for clarity.

Time slows down when awareness sharpens. Everything becomes clearer.

I once cut three recurring meetings from my schedule that weren't producing results.

It felt risky, like I'd lose control.

Instead, I gained hours of focus every week, and my team stepped up to handle what mattered.

The subtraction gave me more progress than any new tool or strategy I could have added.

Every roller coaster I didn't ride became proof that peace is power. Clarity isn't found in the chaos; it's found in stillness.

> *Your peace is worth more than your point.*

Reflection: What could you subtract this week that would create more clarity than any new addition?

CEO POWER MOVES

REFLECT ON THIS CHAPTER

→ Every emotional roller coaster costs energy, and energy is currency.
→ You can't lead with clarity if your nervous system is riding everyone else's highs and lows.
→ Discipline, not motivation, is what carries you through the dips and peaks.
→ Boundaries don't block connection, they preserve your capacity to lead.
→ Subtraction creates progress; every "no" returns power to your focus.
→ Calm is command. The regulated leader sets the tone for every room they walk into.

What is relevant to you now?

_____

_____

_____

STOP LYING TO YOURSELF.

GET REAL.

WRITE IT DOWN.

Which roller coasters show up in your life most often? Work, family, personal?

_____

_____

_____

Where have you been pulled onto a ride you didn't need to take?

_____

_____

_____

Have you ever been just as thrown off by a high just as much as by a low?

_____

_____

_____

How much energy are you spending on rides that aren't yours?

_____

_____

_____

What boundary could return 80% of your clarity this week?

_____

_____

_____

When did motivation fade for you, and did discipline carry you through?

_____

_____

_____

What ride do you secretly enjoy even though it drains you?

_____

_____

_____

ANCHOR - CREATE A NEW HABIT

★ Write down one situation that isn't your roller coaster. Now let it go.
★ Set a boundary sentence: "I care about you, but I'm not getting on your ride."
★ Each morning, name one thing that is your responsibility and commit to it.
★ End the week by asking: Did I stay even keel, or did I burn tickets on someone else's ride?
★ Celebrate one win this week without letting it push you into overconfidence.

Even keel. Clear mind. Energy spent where it compounds. That's the leadership I choose. Every day, when the roller coaster pulls up, I get to make that choice again.

Christopher Amato

Before we move on, here's a great tool:

Every leader operates from an emotional frequency long before they say a word. Your energy is the invisible variable that shapes your leadership, your culture, and ultimately the outcomes you create.

This gauge is a practical adaptation of the work of Dr. David R. Hawkins, whose research in Power vs. Force mapped human consciousness on a scale from low-vibration states like shame and fear to high-vibration states like courage, acceptance, and love.

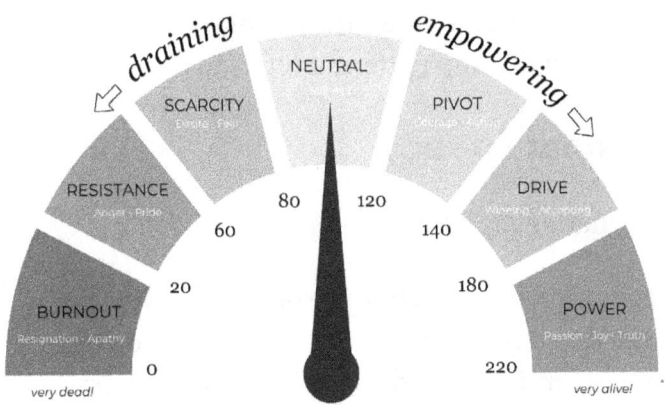

This framework changed the way I understood myself. It gave language to something I had felt my entire life but had never been able to measure: the way my internal state was driving my external results.

When I hit my own collapse, Hawkins' map became both a mirror and a compass. It showed me why certain seasons of my leadership felt heavy, reactive, or chaotic.

It also showed me the path toward clarity, courage, and aligned action. The more I studied it, the clearer it became that CEOs and high-performers needed a version built specifically for the emotional demands of leadership.

That's why I created the CEO Energy Gauge.

Instead of treating "motivation" or "willpower" as the engines of success, this gauge invites you to check the quality of your energy.
Each zone represents a different emotional frequency and the leadership pattern it tends to produce:

Burnout (0–20)

Resignation, apathy, and depletion.

Decisions from this state are often reactive, short-term, or survival-based. This is where many leaders remain until their bodies or circumstances force a reset.

Resistance (20–60)

Anger, frustration, pride.

There is drive here, but it's fueled by pressure, comparison, or emotional reactivity. Productivity is possible, but so is collateral damage.

Scarcity (60–80)

Fear and desire.

This is where leaders push the hardest, often overworking, overthinking, or over-committing in an attempt to stay in control. It "works" temporarily—but at a high cost.

Neutral (80–120)

Stillness. Grounded awareness.

Decisions are cleaner. Emotion does not run the room. From here, leaders regain clarity, access their intuition, and reconnect with what truly matters.

Pivot (120–140)

Courage and action.

The turning point. This is where aligned movement begins and momentum starts to build in the right direction instead of the frantic one.

Drive (140–180)

Confidence, acceptance, willingness.

This is the zone of steady performance, clear thinking, emotional regulation, and strong leadership presence. Cultures thrive when leaders live here.

Power (180–220+)

Joy, truth, passion, service.

This is the highest expression of leadership and power that is felt, not forced. Decisions made here create long-term impact because they come from alignment instead of ego.

This gauge isn't about judging yourself; it's about identifying where you are so you can shift intentionally. Your emotional state is not a personality trait, it's a strategic variable. When you understand where you're operating from, you can lead yourself first, and everyone else better.

This entire book is about rebuilding the internal foundation that allows you to move into the empowering half of the gauge more consistently. When you master your energy, you master your leadership. And when you master your leadership, everything else follows.

CHAPTER 2

Rebuilding An Empire

*"You don't hire for skills,
you hire for attitude.
You can always teach skills."*
— *Simon Sinek*

I remember walking through the facility that evening.

Everyone had gone home. The lights hummed overhead, echoing in the empty space.

I felt the weight of what I had just agreed to. It wasn't excitement, it was gravity. The kind that tells you there's no turning back. I had taken the tiger by the tail, and it was already moving.

The next morning, I called a meeting with the staff. Most of them had been working there for years. They wanted stability more than anything. I told them the truth.

The company was nearly out of money but not out of hope.

That we could make it if we worked together, if we got organized, if we treated every dollar like it mattered. Some believed me. Some just wanted a paycheck. Either way, we started from there.

Vendors were already cutting us off for nonpayment. Payroll was due every two weeks at nearly a quarter of a million dollars. Rent alone was eighty-six thousand a month. The gap between receivables and payables was one point eight million in the negative.

There was no margin for mistakes. I relied on the tools I knew: structure, measurement, negotiation. We tracked everything: production rates, scrap percentages, labor hours, every aspect of productivity and efficiency I could think of. Remembering my fundamental training, "If you can not measure it, you can not manage it".

Numbers became our compass.

I spent days on the floor, nights in the office, weekends strategizing how to renegotiate terms with suppliers who had stopped taking our calls. Slowly, we started to move the needle.

It took sixteen months to pull the company back into the black. Those months felt like years. There were mornings when I questioned whether it was worth it and nights when I didn't sleep at all. Yet every time I thought we had hit the wall, something or someone showed up: a loyal client, a vendor willing to extend terms, a new order that filled a gap just long enough for us to breathe again.

By the end of that run, we were stable. Not thriving yet, but alive. The team had pride again. I did too. For the first time, it felt like all the sacrifice had meaning.

When the company finally steadied, I thought I could exhale. For sixteen months I had lived on caffeine, spreadsheets, and willpower. Now we were solvent again. Orders were coming in. Vendors trusted us. The team was starting to smile when they walked through the door. It felt like the beginning of a new chapter.

Then life reminded me that peace isn't something you arrive at. It's something you have to protect.

As the company found its footing, my personal life began to fracture. It wasn't sudden. It was the slow erosion that happens when one part of your life demands everything and the other parts are left with whatever is left over.

I told myself the long hours and the constant stress were sacrifices for the greater good. Sacrifices for my family. The truth was harder. I had been using work to fill spaces I didn't want to face.

The day the divorce papers were filed, I was sitting in the office reviewing projections. I remember staring at the numbers, trying to make sense of both worlds at once. At work, things finally made sense. At home, nothing did.

Legal advice told me to slow growth, to hold the company steady, but every part of me resisted the idea of stopping. I had just spent more than a year fighting for momentum. To let go of it felt like failure.

I tried to live in two realities at once. During the day I was the CEO driving production, negotiating contracts, holding the vision together. At night I was a man standing in the quiet, wondering how to keep connection alive while everything else was changing.

I split my time between two states, carrying both lives in the same suitcase. Every trip felt like a negotiation between what I had built and what I was trying not to lose.

I told myself to stay strong. I believed that if I held it together long enough, the rest would work itself out. My team needed stability. The people I loved needed reassurance. My lawyer needed documentation (and a lot of money). My vendors needed promises kept.

There wasn't room for breakdowns, so I built a wall around my emotions and kept moving.

Growth was still happening despite the strain. We launched new product lines, attended international trade shows, and expanded our reach into new markets. I remember standing at a booth overseas, watching people handle our products, proud that something we had created was being recognized across the world.

That pride carried me for a while. It was proof that the sacrifices meant something.

When I received the Exporter of the Year award, I should have felt proud. Instead, I felt hollow. The applause was loud, yet inside it was quiet. I was surrounded by people shaking my hand, calling me a success.

None of them knew how many nights I sat awake doing math in my head, wondering how to keep everything from collapsing. I realized then that achievement and peace are not the same thing.

Still, I kept pushing. It was what I knew. The pressure became normal. I convinced myself that this was leadership, staying calm while everything inside me was burning. On the surface, I was winning. Underneath, I was running out of myself.

Loyalty isn't always what it seems.

I once believed that brotherhood was unshakable. I knew for sure that, once given, it was a bond that couldn't break. I poured myself into relationships, business partners, and friendships, convinced that loyalty would be enough to hold everything together.

At that point in my life, I equated loyalty with safety. I thought if I showed up for everyone, if I kept every promise, if I gave more than I got, then the people around me would do the same.

I built partnerships on handshakes, not contracts. I called people "brother" because it felt like a code and mutual understanding that we were building something bigger than ourselves.

Betrayal doesn't always come with an explosion or knife in your back.

Sometimes it comes from a slow leak. Through the slow fade of communication or decisions made behind closed doors while you're still defending the idea of loyalty.

Betrayal doesn't announce itself. It slips in through assumptions, unmet expectations, and hidden agendas. And when it shows up, it cuts deeper than almost anything else.

I remember sitting in my office after a deal collapsed, realizing it wasn't the money that hurt, it was the silence. The avoidance. The people I called brothers, suddenly gone without a word.

I kept replaying the conversations, trying to understand where it went wrong. The truth was, it didn't fall apart overnight. I had ignored the signs for months. The jokes that stung a little too much. The delayed promises.

The energy that shifted when I started speaking more honestly. I wanted to believe the connection was stronger than the cracks. It wasn't. It was already breaking.

That moment forced me to choose between resentment and responsibility. I could keep blaming them, or I could look at why I had stayed in situations that no longer honored the truth.

Betrayal didn't break me, it revealed where I was betraying myself.

Every ounce of attention I spent trying to explain myself, defend myself, or fix what was never mine to fix was energy drained from the work that actually mattered. Betrayal stole focus, scattered my direction, and left me reacting instead of leading.

When you experience betrayal, your mind wants to label it: villain and victim, right and wrong. Those labels begin to establish as beliefs, right or wrong.

Let this sink in:

> *Most betrayal isn't malicious.*
> *It's alignment shifting in real time.*

People change. Values evolve. Priorities move.

The energy that once connected you no longer fits who you're becoming, and that friction exposes everything that's out of integrity.

Weak boundaries made it worse. I wanted so badly to keep the connection alive that I kept giving ground, excusing behavior, and over-explaining my decisions. I thought that was loyalty. It wasn't. It was avoidance that was eroding the foundation I was creating.

Avoidance doesn't stop pain. It multiplies it. Every time I stayed silent when something didn't feel right, I was training people to ignore my truth.

Every time I made myself smaller to keep the peace, I was teaching others how to treat me. The moment I realized that was the moment everything shifted.

Boundaries are leadership.

The moment I drew the line, the moment I stopped bleeding energy into relationships that no longer honored truth, clarity returned.

Boundaries don't make you hard. They make you clear. They show you where the door is and where the key is to unlock it.

STRONG BOUNDARIES DON'T REPEL THE RIGHT PEOPLE, THEY REPEL THE WRONG ONES.

When betrayal happens, boundaries prevent it from becoming a total collapse. They become the frame that keeps you steady while the emotions settle.

I learned that boundaries don't end relationships. They do reveal which ones are real, then we get to decide what to do with that data.

The people who are meant to walk beside you will respect your boundaries and not take them personally. The ones who aren't your people will push against them until they break. Either way, truth still wins.

The hardest lesson of betrayal is this: trust is sacred, but it is not guaranteed. When it breaks, you can waste years trying to hold together something that's already gone, or you can learn the deeper truth.

Loyalty without alignment is a liability.

When you start aligning with truth, something beautiful happens. You stop chasing connection and start attracting it. The right people show up when you stop settling for the wrong ones.

CEO POWER MOVES

REFLECT ON THIS CHAPTER

→ Betrayal doesn't always break you, sometimes it frees you.
→ Energy leaks through defending, explaining, and fixing what isn't yours.
→ Avoidance disguised as loyalty will drain you dry.
→ Boundaries create respect. They protect energy and clarify alignment.
→ Brotherhood without alignment is just a shared illusion.
→ True loyalty is built on mutual integrity, not shared history.

What is relevant to you now?

_____

_____

_____

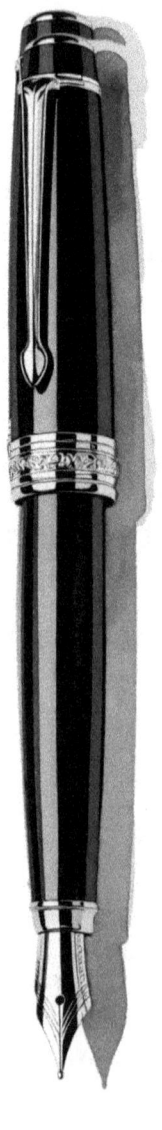

STOP LYING TO YOURSELF.
GET REAL. WRITE IT DOWN.

Where in your life are you mistaking loyalty for fear of loss?

_____

_____

_____

_____

Who drains your energy the moment you get honest with them?

_____

_____

_____

_____

What truth have you been avoiding to keep the peace?

_____

_____

Christopher Amato

How do your current boundaries protect your peace, or fall short?

_____

_____

_____

What would it look like to trust yourself the same way you once trusted others?

_____

_____

_____

If loyalty is sacred, what must it be built on?

_____

_____

_____

What red flags have you missed in the past and learned from?

_____

_____

_____

ANCHOR - CREATE A NEW HABIT

★ Identify one place where you've been over-explaining, then stop it.

★ Write one boundary sentence that protects your energy.

★ Replace one "fix-it" moment with silence and observation.

★ Practice saying "no" to one situation that no longer aligns.

Even in betrayal, there's clarity.
When you stop betraying yourself, the right people can finally stay.

CHAPTER 3

The Betrayal

"Loyalty without alignment is a liability."
                                    Christopher Amato

T he slowdown started quietly.

A few clients ordered less than usual. Then more followed.

I told myself it was seasonal, that markets shift, that we would make it up next quarter.

Down deep, I knew something wasn't right. Patterns that had always been steady began to fade, and I could feel the pulse of the company changing.

For months I pushed forward, hoping hard work would correct what data couldn't explain. Then I learned what was really happening.

The person I had trusted most inside the company, who knew every formula, every vendor, every process, had taken what we built and walked it out the door.

He copied the proprietary formulas, the vendor lists, and the production methods that kept our clients connected to us. He handed them to another operation and offered my customers a way to continue without me.

When I discovered it, the truth landed like a weight on my chest. It wasn't just the money. It was the realization that I had built so much on trust that wasn't mutual.

In a few months, sixty-five percent of our revenue disappeared. Machines sat silent. Payroll bills waited with no clear path to meet them. The rent was still eighty-six thousand a month.

We had done nothing wrong on paper, yet the foundation was gone.

I spent nights going through every computer record, every file. The evidence was there in thousands of screenshots and emails my security system had recorded.

I brought it to counsel, ready to fight. The attorney listened carefully, then explained the math of justice.

The retainer alone would exceed what we could recover. The man who took it had no assets to cover a judgment. I sat there realizing that truth doesn't always equal fairness.

We turned to the authorities and sought to fight in civil court attempting to get some form of justice. For more than a year I worked with investigators, building the case, organizing proof, believing that right would win if I just stayed patient. We even secured access to his personal email account and confirmed everything we already knew.

When the file was complete, we delivered it to the attorney general's office. A new administration had just taken over. They reviewed it and declined to prosecute. Intellectual property, they said, was too complicated. It wasn't theft in the traditional sense.

I left that meeting numb. A year and a half of work, evidence, and hope gone in a paragraph of legal language. There was no one to blame. The system was doing what it does.

Christopher Amato

I had to decide whether I would spend the rest of my energy on anger or on rebuilding.

That night I sat alone in the office long after everyone left. The machines were still, the air heavy with uncertainty and silence. I thought about everything I had carried, everything I had lost, and what it had cost to keep pretending I could control it all.

The betrayal hurt, yet beneath it was another truth I couldn't ignore:

I had created a culture that relied on trust without enough structure to protect it. I had assumed loyalty would match intention.

It rarely does.

I went back to work. Not out of pride, but because I wasn't done learning. I traveled again, met new clients, attended trade shows, and did everything I could to rebuild. It was slower this time, more deliberate.

I no longer believed in the myth of invincibility. I believed in showing up, even when it hurt.

Resilience changed shape for me then. It stopped being about how fast I could recover and started being about how honest I could be while doing it. Some lessons arrive disguised as loss.

This one came wearing a name badge and a company logo, but its purpose was spiritual. It taught me that leadership *without humility eventually breaks under its own weight. I had to learn how to lead with both.*

Looking back - Lessons from the Rubble

From the street, everything looked intact. Inside, the cracks ran deep.

I built things the way I was taught: add more, move faster, push harder. If a problem surfaced, hire someone, schedule another meeting, launch another initiative.

We chased balance like a target we could hit if we just worked long enough. The illusion of balance is exactly that, an illusion. You do not balance everything.

> ***You prioritize what matters and accept the trade-offs.***

The slow corrosion happened where no one was watching. I was proud of how busy we were. Schedules overflowing, back-to-back calls, a full calendar stamped like proof that we mattered.

What destroyed us was not one event. It was a steady leak of energy.

Small, consistent withdrawals. A yes that should have been a no. One more explanation that was unnecessary. Rescuing an unaligned project out of guilt.

Each leak was minor on its own, and together they drained the system, first financially, then energetically.

Inside the empire, my nervous system had been hijacked by habit. I reacted to the urgent instead of the important. Scattered energy produced scattered results.

The organization mirrored me. Messy inside, messy outside. When your inner world is chaotic, your outer systems follow.

A-HA MOMENT!
Think of every situation like a water balloon.
If it has small holes in it, when you begin to pour water in, the small leaks begin to appear and water leaks out.
If you don't seal the holes, pouring more water in just rips it open faster.
You get into a race to pour more water in the top than what is leaking out the bottom.
A race you will never win.
Burnout isn't from lack of hustle; it's from trying to outwork the holes.

Rebuilds start with subtraction.

Real growth is not adding more, it is removing what pulls you away from your axis.

Subtraction is unpopular because it asks you to let go of accepted measures of success. Billable hours, vanity metrics, and the exhausted glow of being indispensable are false currencies.

Subtraction creates space for clarity, rhythm and to do what actually matters.

The collapse taught me a harder truth: you do not control outcomes, you control inputs. You cannot micromanage fortune. You can only steward your state.

When your nervous system is regulated, your leadership becomes a signal, a frequency, not noise. When it is not, everything you touch becomes unstable and like static.

So when an empire crumbles, do not romanticize the fall. Name it. Own it. Clean up the mess.

Then slowly, intentionally, subtract. Build anchors, not weights. Prioritize what carries the most meaning. Leadership is not about balance. It is about choosing what to carry and what to release.

The KPIs nobody tracks but every CEO should:

- Time spent avoiding hard conversations
- Number of "yeses" I should've said no to
- Hours lost to emotional reactivity
- Emotional debt accumulated

CEO POWER MOVES

REFLECT ON THIS CHAPTER

→ Empires decay from internal rot, not external attacks.
→ Busy ≠ effective. Activity does not equal alignment.
→ Energy leaks — small, repeated drains — create burnout and failure.
→ Messy inside = messy outside; inner order leads to outer order.
→ Subtraction is strategy: remove what drains you to create space for what matters.
→ You control inputs (energy, boundaries, priorities), not outcomes.

What is relevant to you now?

_____

_____

_____

STOP LYING TO YOURSELF. GET REAL. WRITE IT DOWN.

Where do small cracks show up in your world that you keep ignoring?

_____

_____

_____

What are the habits that look productive but quietly corrode your foundation?

_____

_____

_____

Which responsibilities are truly yours, and which ones are distractions?

_____

_____

_____

How much of your identity is tied to "busy"?

_____

_____

_____

List a few things you do that are "busy work" that wouldn't matter if they never got done?

_____

_____

_____

_____

_____

What could you remove this week that would return energy to what matters most?

_____

_____

_____

_____

_____

ANCHOR - CREATE A NEW HABIT

★ Identify one recurring energy leak and close it.

★ Schedule an hour each morning with no noise, no email, no phone, to let clarity surface.

★ Replace one measure of success with one measure of peace.

★ End each day asking, Did I harness energy or allow the static and noise to rule the day?

Even in ruin, the foundation can teach you. The cracks only expose what needs strengthening. Every rebuild begins in silence, with subtraction, and with the decision to stand back up.

Christopher Amato

PART TWO

THE DESCENT

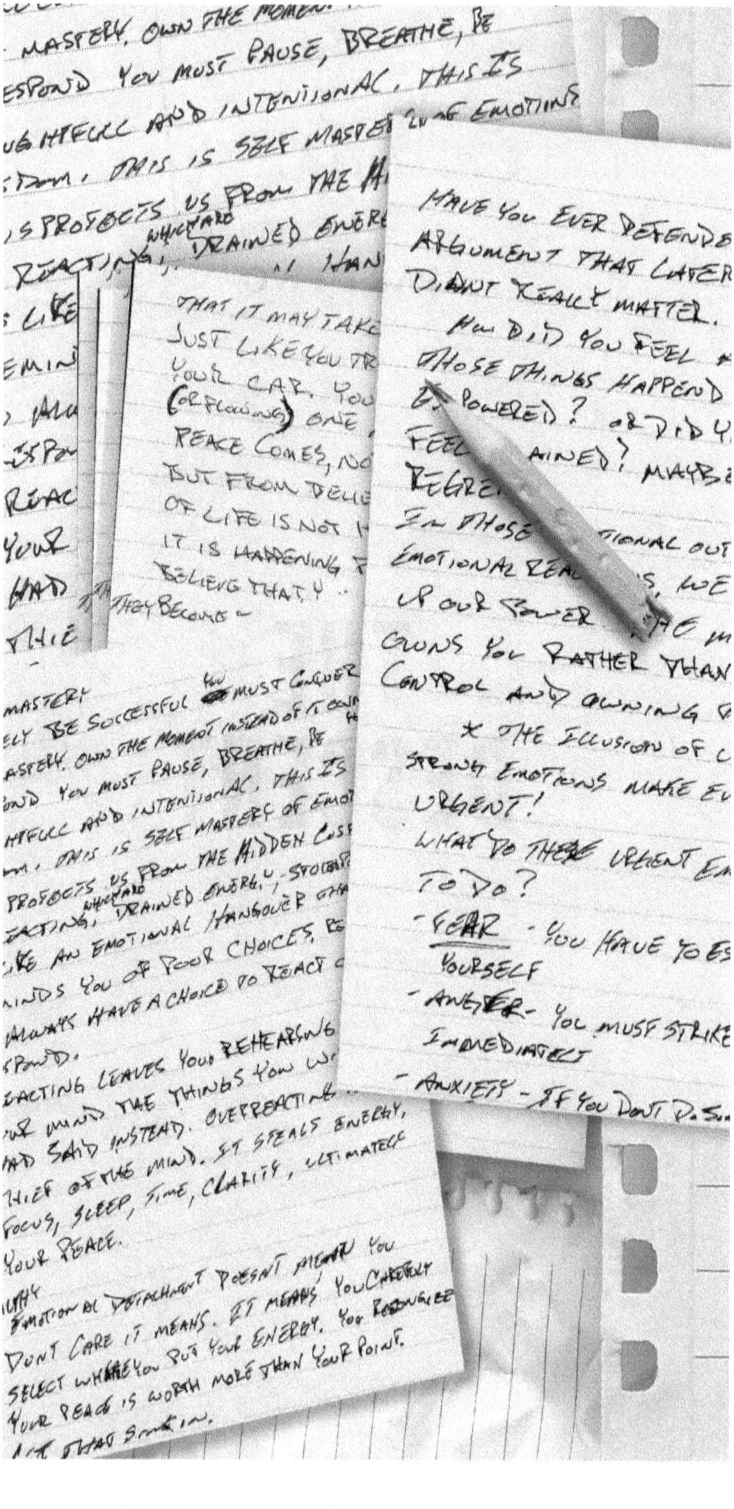

[Top page - partially visible]
...MASTERY, OWN THE MOMEN...
...ESPOND YOU MUST PAUSE, BREATHE, BE
...UGHTFULL AND INTENTIONAL. THIS IS
...TRY. THIS IS SELF MASTERY ... OF EMOTION?
...S PROTECTS US FROM THE H...
                WHICH ARE
...REACTING,   DRAINED ENER...
...LIKE   ... HAN...
...EMIN...
...PAU...
...-S PO...
...REAC...
...YOUR...
...HAD   ...
...THEY BECOME ~
...THIE...

[Middle small page]
THAT IT MAY TAKE
JUST LIKE YOU TR...
YOUR CAR. YOU ...
(OR FLOWING) ONE ...
PEACE COMES, NO...
BUT FROM DELI...
OF LIFE IS NOT H...
IT IS HAPPENING ...
BELIEVE THAT Y...

[Right page]
HAVE YOU EVER DEFENDE...
ARGUMENT THAT LATER ...
DIDN'T REALLY MATTER.
   HOW DID YOU FEEL ...
THOSE THINGS HAPPEND
EMPOWERED? OR DID Y...
FEEL ...AINED? MAYBE ...
REGRE...
IN THOSE ... TIONAL OUT...
EMOTIONAL REA... S, WE ...
UP OUR POWER ... THE M...
OWNS YOU RATHER THAN ...
CONTROL AND OWNING ...
  * THE ILLUSION OF U...
STRONG EMOTIONS MAKE EV...
URGENT!
WHAT DO THESE URGENT E...
TO DO?
- FEAR - YOU HAVE TO ES...
  YOURSELF
- ANGER - YOU MUST STRIKE
  IMMEDIATELY
- ANXIETY - IF YOU DON'T D.S...

[Lower left page]
MASTERY
...LY BE SUCCESSFUL YOU MUST CONQUER ...
...ASTERY. OWN THE MOMENT INSTEAD OF IT OWN...
...OND YOU MUST PAUSE, BREATHE, BE
...HTFULL AND INTENTIONAL. THIS IS
...M. THIS IS SELF MASTERY OF EMOT...
...PROTECTS US FROM THE HIDDEN COST...
           WHICH ARE
...ACTING, DRAINED ENERGY, STOLEN ...
...KE AN EMOTIONAL HANGOVER THA...
...INDS YOU OF POOR CHOICES. RE...
...ALWAYS HAVE A CHOICE TO REACT O...
...SPOND.
...ACTING LEAVES YOU REHEARSING
...UR MIND THE THINGS YOU W...
...HAD SAID INSTEAD. OVERREACTING ...
...HIEF OF THE MIND. IT STEALS ENERGY,
...FOCUS, SLEEP, TIME, CLARITY, ULTIMATELY
...YOUR PEACE.

[Bottom page]
...LTHY
...EMOTIONAL DETACHMENT DOESN'T MEAN YOU
...DON'T CARE. IT MEANS YOU CAREFULLY
...SELECT WHERE YOU PUT YOUR ENERGY. YOU RECOGNIZE
...YOUR PEACE IS WORTH MORE THAN YOUR POINT.
...ALL THAT S...H IN.

CHAPTER 4

When The Empire Crumbles

"Failure is simply the opportunity to begin again, this time more intelligently."

Henry Ford

The attorney general refused to prosecute.

I stopped waiting for someone else to make things right. It was clear that no one was coming to fix it. If the company was going to survive, it would have to be through my own persistence. So I went back to work.

I doubled down on the trade shows, the outreach, the conversations that could lead to new business. Every morning I walked the production floor, greeting people by name, reminding them that we still had a future. I refused to let despair take root.

Somewhere between exhaustion and determination, a kind of faith began to form, a quiet belief that doing the next right thing would be enough.

For a moment that faith paid off. We secured a four-million-dollar production contract with a publicly traded company. It was the kind of deal that could reset everything. A full year of production, guaranteed revenue, a way to pay down debt and rebuild the team's confidence. For the first time in a long while, I felt momentum turning back in our favor.

Then the call came from the landlord. Our five-year lease was ending, and the property had been sold to a real-estate investment trust. We had been late on rent before, always catching up, always finding a way.

The new owners didn't want stories or promises. They wanted numbers that balanced on a spreadsheet.

They demanded a five-year lease renewal at eighty-six thousand dollars a month and insisted that a third party, not me, not the company, personally guarantee the entire amount. More than five million dollars in rent over the term.

I explained the new contract, the stability it offered, and even arranged a call between the fund manager of the REIT and the CEO who had just awarded us the order. That CEO offered to pay the rent directly out of the production payments. It was the most practical solution imaginable.

They declined. They didn't want a one-year bridge. They wanted a long-term guarantee they could record as predictable income. It was business, not cruelty. The realization still hurt.

I had done everything right, rebuilt from every setback, stayed honest, stayed accountable, yet the decision rested with people who didn't even know my name. We were nothing more than a line item on their balance sheet.

When the call ended, I sat in silence. My hands were still on the desk, my heart somewhere between anger and relief. Anger because I had fought so hard for so long. Relief because deep down I knew I was at the end of what sheer willpower could do and inside I was mentally, physically and emotionally exhausted

The company wasn't failing from neglect or incompetence. It was being released. Life was closing a chapter I kept trying to rewrite.

Christopher Amato

Bankruptcy followed. There were forms, signatures, inventories of assets, and the dismantling of what had once been a living thing. Employees moved on. Clients found new suppliers. I stayed until the lights were turned off for the last time.

Standing in that empty building, I felt grief, but I also felt something I hadn't in years.

Stillness.

That stillness became a teacher. It asked questions I had avoided: Who am I when there is nothing left to manage? What is leadership when no one is watching? What if losing everything isn't punishment but permission?

The collapse stripped me bare.

Without the titles and pressure, I could finally see the patterns I had mistaken for purpose. The late nights, the endless motion, the constant proving.

All of it had been an armor that kept me from feeling what I needed to face. Beneath the wreckage was a man learning how to listen again. Learning how to breathe without a deadline. Learning that success without peace isn't success at all.

The company died on paper, yet something in me came alive. What ended in bankruptcy began in awareness. That awareness became the foundation for everything that came next.

...NGS) ONE S...
PEACE COMES, NOT ...OUR S...
BUT FROM DELI... FU...
OF LIFE IS NOT...
T IS HAPP... THA...
BELIEVE TH... PPENING
COME TO ... FOR YOU!
... YOUR LOSSES, U
... TEACH...

YOUR MIND IS THERE TO PROTECT
YOU. IT TRY'S TO TELL THE FUTURE
TO HOPEFULLY AVOID THINGS THAT
WOULD HARM YOU. BRING YOU
SADNESS OR PAIN. YOUR MIND
ALWAY WANTS YOU TO FOLLOW THE
LIGHT BUT WHERE IS FAITH
AND TRUST IN THE PROCESS? IF
IT IS LIGHT AND YOU CAN SEE IT,
THERE IS NO NEED TO HAVE FAITH
FAITH IS IN THE UNSEEN. IT IS
IN THE DARKNESS, IN THE SHADOW
WHERE THE MIND BRINGS FEAR.
THE TRUTH IS, WE MUST STEP INT
THE DARKNESS, NOT KNOWING W...
IT MAY LEAD. LET THE MIND GO.
GIVE IT PERMISSION TO RELEASE ...
PROTECTIVE RESPONSIBILITY AND G...
INTO THE RIVER OF LIFE, STEP
THE FLOW, SEEING AND KNOW...
... BUT ALLOW...

CEO POWER MOVES

REFLECT ON THIS CHAPTER

→ Collapse isn't always failure; sometimes it's a signal for correction.
→ What you built can become what blinds you.
→ Endings reveal where force replaced flow.
→ Control is not leadership; awareness is.
→ When the structure falls, you finally see what was holding it up—fear, habit, or truth.
→ Stillness after loss is not emptiness; it's the space where alignment begins again.

What is relevant to you now?

_____

_____

_____

_____

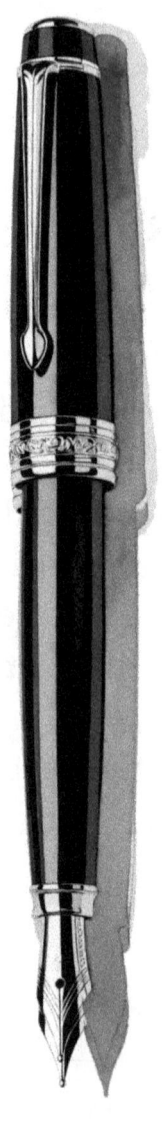

STOP LYING TO YOURSELF.
GET REAL. WRITE IT DOWN.

Where are you forcing outcomes instead of following what's real?

_____

_____

_____

What stories keep you rebuilding what needs to be released?

_____

_____

_____

Who would you be without the title, the role, or the company name?

_____

_____

_____

_____

What part of you still believes effort equals worth?

_____

_____

_____

What truth have you been too busy to feel?

_____

_____

_____

_____

What do you know about yourself that you are afraid to have seen by others?

_____

_____

_____

_____

_____

ANCHOR – CREATE A NEW HABIT

★ Stop fixing what's ending. Let one thing die that's asking to.
★ Replace one hour of problem-solving with one hour of silence.
★ Journal what remains when nothing external defines you.
★ Practice gratitude for what collapsed. It's clearing space for integrity.
★ Before you rebuild, breathe. The next empire will rise from what stayed honest in the fall.

Even in collapse, there is clarity. What falls apart reveals what was never meant to stand. Leadership begins again in the silence after the storm, when identity is stripped bare, and only truth remains.

Christopher Amato

CHAPTER 5

The Journey Down

"It's through curiosity and looking at opportunities in new ways that we've always mapped our path."

Michael Dell

E*viction notices started showing up on my door.*

Threats to change the locks. Warnings that production would be shut down. All of it hit at once. I kept showing up as the CEO, answering phones, steadying my voice, trying to solve what felt unsolvable.

Because the landlord refused the offer from the publicly traded company to pay our rent directly, the lease expired. We were still operating in the building without a contract when a demand letter arrived. Thirty days to vacate.

I read the notice over and over. Now what? I racked my brain for options.

So many times I was able to come up with some miraculous solution that kept me in the game. For many months now I literally felt like a magician, I pulled rabbit after rabbit out of a hat. However this time I went to the hat and it was empty. I filed for bankruptcy reorganization to buy time.

It paused the eviction and gave me a thin window to find another solution. The guarantor never materialized. Reorganization shifted to liquidation.

Receivership followed. A court-appointed CPA took control. I was locked out of my own company and informed that I was no longer needed. The debt I had personally guaranteed remained my responsibility.

I had no revenue, no authority, and no way to keep the promises I had made to everyone who counted on me. That was the day the title came off and the man underneath had to meet himself.

On a shelf behind me sat trophies and framed certificates. CEO of the Year. Exporter of the Year. Photos from trade shows in Dubai, Italy, Hong Kong, South Korea, Japan.

I looked at them and felt nothing. The identity I had built was gone. I reached for the next thing, tried to broker deals, tried to pivot into a different business. I did it without healing the shock and grief inside me, which meant I did it from fear. Deals created in fear invite more of the same. The results proved it.

By 2020 the numbers told the truth. More than three million dollars lost in the bankruptcy. Savings gone. Then the world shut down. Investors went silent. Hiring froze. I sent out hundreds of resumes and heard the same response. Overqualified. A flight risk. Positions above my level were not being filled. The mailbox stayed empty.

In 2021 I checked my account and saw twenty-four cents. I stopped leaving the house. I stopped taking calls. I could not find a reason to keep pretending I was fine.

Depression settled over everything. I recognized that I was not safe with myself and walked into a crisis clinic. I asked for help.

They gave me a chair, a schedule, and a chance.

Medications were introduced to stabilize my mind. They quieted the storm but also quieted everything else.

My thoughts moved through fog.

The world lost color. I was no longer at risk, yet I felt numb to my own life. Once I had enough stability to think clearly, I chose a different path with my doctor.

We tapered off, slowly and carefully. The fog lifted. The hurt was still there, which meant I could finally face it.

I entered a new relationship while I was still unhealed. At first it felt like relief. Over time it revealed itself as control, criticism, and manipulation.

I tolerated what I should have confronted because the part of me that felt unworthy believed I had to earn love. That season became a mirror. It showed me how easily I could abandon myself if I did not learn to stand up for my own heart.

No one chooses collapse.

No one signs up for betrayal, burnout, or brokenness.
Once the cracks appear, you face a choice: deny the descent and keep running, or step into it and allow it to change you.

I used to think leadership was about control: control the market, control the outcomes, control the people. Yet the myth of control always exposes itself.

You only control inputs. You control your energy, your focus, your state. Those inputs shape everything else.

The descent is not about failure. It is about alignment. Misalignment costs more than any mistake you could ever make. It drains energy, destroys clarity, and corrodes trust.

Alignment, even when it is painful, produces compound returns. It restores clarity. It rebuilds conviction.

Aligned leaders last.

The ego hates this.

It will convince you that slowing down means losing, that surrender is weakness, that descent is death.

Ego is just a system running on low power mode. The more you inflate it, the more energy drains, and the less clarity you have to hear the truth.

Reduce ego, preserve energy.

Preserve authentic energy, and connection to Source opens.

That is where the downloads come from, not when you are scrambling to hold the illusion of control, but when you let go enough to receive.

Christopher Amato

Pain as a teacher

For most of my life, I thought I could outwork pain. Out-think it. Out-strategize it. If I could keep moving, if I could fill the schedule and silence the noise with progress, maybe the ache would fade into the background.

It never did.

Pain waits.

It does not care how many titles you earn, how many dollars you add to your balance sheet, or how many people call you "successful." If it is not faced, it waits in the shadows. When you least expect it, it demands payment.

Facing the Pain

Here's the truth: shifts do not just happen. Alignment does not fall out of the sky. You cannot slap discipline on top of a fractured nervous system and expect power. Internal alignment has to come first. That means facing what you have been running from.

Your nervous system will always speak before your logic does. If it is dysregulated, fear will speak first. Anger will speak first. Anxiety will speak first.

You may not even realize it is your body talking, not your soul. When that unregulated system leads, your decisions reflect chaos, not clarity. The only way through is to slow down, silence the noise and listen.

Breath is the bridge.

Every day your body breathes without thought, your subconscious running the system in the background.

The moment you take control of your breath deliberately, intentionally, you connect the subconscious with the conscious. You interrupt the autopilot.

You regulate the storm.

In that regulation, you open yourself to guidance. Downloads do not come while thrashing in the water. They come when you are quiet enough to hear them even in the midst of the storm. Breath slows the spin, calms the chaos, and connects you to Source.

Pain is not conquered by grinding harder. It is transformed by recognizing, pausing, regulating, and surrendering.

When you stop trying to be smarter than your pain and finally give it your attention, you become wiser because of it.

CEO POWER MOVES

REFLECT ON THIS CHAPTER

- → Pain ignored does not disappear; it waits until you face it.
- → Shifts do not happen by force; internal alignment comes first.
- → The nervous system speaks before the mind; regulate it or chaos will lead.
- → Breath is the bridge between the conscious and subconscious.
- → Stillness opens the channel for guidance and clarity.

What is relevant to you now?

_____

_____

_____

_____

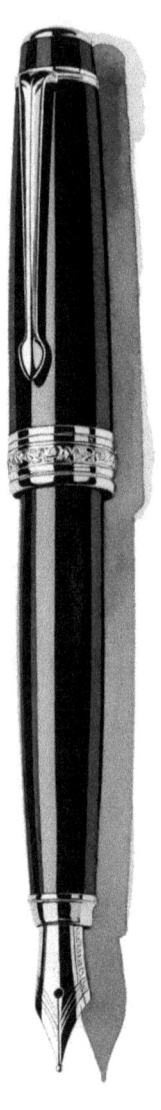

STOP LYING TO YOURSELF. GET REAL. WRITE IT DOWN.

What pain are you still trying to outwork or outthink?

_____

_____

_____

Where does fear speak louder than truth in your decisions?

_____

_____

_____

Where in your life can you begin to pause long enough to listen before acting?

_____

_____

_____

What do you think about breath work, and focused breathing exercises?

_____

_____

_____

What would change if you treated breathwork like a business meeting with your soul?

_____

_____

_____

In what arena can you begin to recognize the difference between numbing and healing in your own habits?

_____

_____

_____

_____

_____

_____

ANCHOR - CREATE A NEW HABIT

★ Begin each morning with deliberate breathing techniques before checking your phone, email or social media.

★ When tension hits, pause and notice what part of your body speaks first.

★ Replace one act of numbing with one act of presence.

★ Each night, ask yourself: Did I respond from fear or from peace today?

Every descent carries the seed of awakening. The pain you finally face becomes the doorway to your next level of strength.

Christopher Amato

CHAPTER 6

Facing The Darkness

"The greatest danger in times of turbulence is not the turbulence, it is to act with yesterday's logic."

Peter Drucker

Healing arrived in phases.

First I stabilized. Then I listened. Then I told the truth to myself. I began the shadow work I had avoided.

Childhood patterns. Old agreements. The places where I had confused overgiving with love. The part of me that needed constant achievement to feel safe.

I learned that choosing myself is not selfish. It is stewardship. When I could finally say no, I could finally say yes to a life that fit the man I am becoming.

I released the relationship that mirrored my wounds. I kept the lesson. I rebuilt simple rhythms.

Sleep. Food. Movement. Prayer.

Honest conversation with a small circle who would not let me lie to myself. A local clinic supported me for months and asked for nothing in return. Their generosity still humbles me. With their help, I remembered what I had already learned in better times and began to live it again.

I once believed resilience meant pushing through pain. Now I understand it begins with presence. The collapse removed what was false. The descent taught me how to stay with what is true. That choice changed everything.

Every collapse leaves a silence. Mine lasted months. In that stillness I realized I had been trying to rebuild from the outside in. Success, relationships, identity. All of it had been architecture without a foundation.

I had to stop measuring progress by what I could restore and start measuring it by how honest I could be with myself. The healing began when I stopped asking what I had lost and started remembering who I was meant to become.

That question didn't rebuild the company. It rebuilt me.

Radical ownership

There comes a point when you realize

The biggest enemy isn't out there, it's in here.

The skeletons do not parade themselves in daylight. They live in the shadows, unspoken regrets, failures you buried, and the parts of yourself you swore you would never let anyone see.

They are not gone. They are waiting.

Until you face them, they haunt every boardroom, every relationship, every decision. They will show up quietly at first, then increase in intensity until you give them the attention they need.

Choosing Surrender

There was a night when I finally stopped fighting. The house was quiet. The phone was silent. I sat alone and realized that every attempt to force control had failed.

Nothing left to fix. Nothing left to prove.

I remember breathing, really breathing, for the first time in months.

The grief came in waves.

Loss of business, loss of family, loss of identity. I let it come. I stopped resisting. There was a strange peace in the breakdown, like something greater had been waiting for me to stop long enough to listen.

For the first time, I asked a question I had never asked before:

"What if this is not punishment? What if this is initiation?"

That question changed everything.

The descent stopped feeling like death and started feeling like birth. I was not being destroyed. I was being rebuilt. I was remembering who I was created to be.

Lessons from the River

Descent is a choice because surrender is a choice. The river of life is not there to drown you. It is there to carry you into alignment if you stop fighting the current.

Letting go does not mean drifting into doom.

Letting go means trusting the flow to bring you to the exact place you are meant to be.

When you choose the flow, you surrender to transformation.

Pain becomes a teacher.
Stillness becomes strength.
Alignment becomes your compass.
Collapse becomes the threshold of something new.

Faith & Flow

Your mind is there to protect you.

It tries to predict the future to avoid pain or disappointment. It wants to shield you from darkness, yet in doing so, it keeps you from faith. Faith lives in the unseen. It lives in surrender.

When you stop demanding control and let yourself drift into the river of life, you trade panic for peace. You do not need to know every turn. You only need to trust that the current knows the way.

Peace does not come from knowing. It comes from believing that life is not happening to you, it is happening through you, it is happening for you.

When you finally ask, "What is this trying to teach me?" the current begins to carry you again.

Light Noise

The first time I understood light noise was in a hot tub on the Island of Roatan.
At first, the stars looked faint, ordinary, maybe a few scattered points in the darkness. Then someone turned off the lights in the house.

In an instant, the Milky Way appeared.

Thousands of stars, brilliant and alive, had been there all along. I just couldn't see them through the glare of the light noise.

That's what ego does.

It floods your inner world with artificial brightness: the need to prove, to perform, to stay visible when what you really need is darkness.

Light noise
keeps you busy.
Presence turns it off.

The quieter I let my life become, the more truth I could see. Peace. Presence. Purpose. All of it had been there the whole time, waiting for the lights to go out.

Lessons from the Dark

Energy is identity. You do not attract what you want; you attract what you are. Stillness is strength because it takes more courage to sit with yourself than to sprint past yourself.

The nervous system remains the compass.

When it is regulated, it leads you home.

The descent is not punishment. It is purification. Skeletons lose their power when they are seen. Darkness loses its grip when you bring light to it.

Christopher Amato

CEO POWER MOVES

REFLECT ON THIS CHAPTER

→ The greatest enemies are the skeletons inside, not the critics outside.
→ Energy is identity. You attract what you are, not what you wish for.
→ Stillness is strength; it reveals the truth beneath the noise.
→ Inner chaos creates outer chaos; alignment begins within.
→ Focused attention exposes what distraction keeps hidden.
→ Faith lives in surrender, not in control.

What is relevant to you now?

_____

_____

_____

_____

STOP LYING TO YOURSELF.
GET REAL. WRITE IT DOWN.

Which skeletons still whisper in your decisions today?

_____

_____

_____

How often do you confuse distraction for safety?

_____

_____

What truth would surface if you let silence stay long enough to hear it?

_____

_____

_____

Where in your life is ego creating light noise?

_____

_____

_____

What artificial light can you turn off this week so you can see more clearly?

_____

_____

_____

_____

_____

In what area can you trust the current when you cannot see the destination?

_____

_____

_____

_____

ANCHOR - CREATE A NEW HABIT

★ Schedule ten minutes of stillness with no phone, no music, and no task.

★ Write down one recurring fear and ask, What is this teaching me?

★ Remove one artificial light from your life —a distraction, a habit, or a performance.

★ Each night, thank one shadow for what it revealed today.

The descent is the invitation.
The darkness was never the enemy.
It was the teacher waiting for your attention.

PART THREE

THE REBUILD

CHAPTER 7

The Winding Road To Wholeness

"The moment you stop learning is the moment you stop leading."
Jack Welch, Former CEO of GE

Healing was never a straight line.

After I ended the difficult relationship that mirrored my wounds, I stepped carefully into another one. It was healthier, kinder, and taught me what partnership could look like when two people are growing.

We cared for each other, yet the timing wasn't right. Even that ending carried grace. It showed me how far I had come from the man who once accepted pain as proof of love.

When that relationship ended, I knew I couldn't just move forward. I had to look at myself even more deeply. There were still subtle, familiar patterns that kept repeating under new faces and new circumstances.

I began another round of work, this time without denial, without rushing to rebuild anything external. The focus was simple: take radical responsibility for what I attract, what I tolerate, and what I choose.

That inner work changed everything.

For the first time in years, I wasn't trying to fix anyone. I was building from peace instead of from pressure.

My work began to shift with me. Ideas that had been dormant started to move again. Opportunities returned, not through force, but through alignment.

The people showing up in my world reflected the energy I had finally learned to hold—steady, grounded, open.

Then someone new came into my life, and it felt different from the beginning. No performance. No rescue missions. Just honesty and ease. Partnership, not dependency.

Together we are building something real, something that grows because we do. It's a reminder that love doesn't arrive to complete you. It meets you once you remember who you are.

The same is true for business. The more I learned to lead from clarity rather than fear, the more everything around me began to respond.

Doors opened. Conversations led to collaborations. Projects that once seemed impossible started to flow again. It wasn't luck. It was resonance.

When you stop chasing what you think you deserve and start living as the person you already are, life adjusts to meet you there.

That's what this story has always been about. Not failure. Not success. Integration. The collapse gave me humility. The healing gave me depth.

The rebuilding gave me a choice. I don't measure success by revenue anymore. I measure it by peace. And by that standard, I'm finally wealthier than I have ever been.

Christopher Amato

The Challenge of the Healed

Hurt people unconsciously hurt people.
Healed people consciously want to heal people.

Once healing begins, awareness sharpens.

You start to see the pain in others instead of reacting to their behavior.

Their words, their anger, their projection, you recognize it as a reflection of wounds they have not yet faced. Empathy replaces judgment. Yet this awakening comes with a new challenge.

The healed often want to accelerate the healing of others.

It feels loving, yet it is a desire to control in disguise.

You cannot force transformation any more than you can pull open the petals of a flower before it is ready to bloom. What opens too soon will not thrive.

You cannot heal someone's journey.

You can only hold space, trust the process, and model what healed looks like. That is leadership at its highest level, not fixing, but embodying.

The same fire that warms can also destroy.

When your energy burns too hot, even with good intentions, it can scorch what you are trying to nurture.

The lesson is patience.

The healed lead not through force but through presence.

Trust that everyone's journey unfolds at its own pace. Your responsibility is not to rush it, but to remain grounded enough to remind others that healing is possible because they can see it in you.

CEO POWER MOVES

REFLECT ON THIS CHAPTER

- → You do not control outcomes; you control inputs: energy, focus, and state.
- → Misalignment costs more than mistakes; alignment creates compound returns.
- → Ego in control equals low power mode; humility restores energy and clarity.
- → Surrender is not weakness; it is the doorway to Source.
- → Healing cannot be forced; it unfolds through patience and example.
- → Descent is transformation when you choose to let go.

What is relevant to you now?

_____

_____

_____

_____

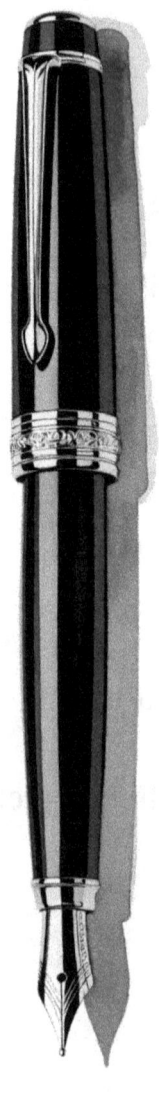

STOP LYING TO YOURSELF. GET REAL. WRITE IT DOWN.

Where are you still trying to control what needs to be surrendered?

_____

_____

_____

Who in your world are you expecting to heal or grow before they are ready?

_____

_____

_____

How would your energy change if you released the illusion of control?

_____

_____

_____

What does surrender look like in your leadership, your family, or your faith?

Who do you trust completely that you can surrender to?

Can you trust that descent is the path to alignment, not destruction?

What are you afraid to look into in your own descent?

ANCHOR - CREATE A NEW HABIT

★ When control impulses appear, pause and breathe before acting.

★ Identify one area where you can replace effort with trust.

★ If you want to help someone heal, focus on your own presence first.

★ End each day by writing one thing you released instead of forced

---

The descent is not the end. It is the initiation. When you stop fighting the river, you realize it was always carrying you home.

Christopher Amato

CHAPTER 8

Forgiving Myself For Causing Pain

"Before you are a leader, success is all about growing yourself. When you become a leader, success is all about growing others."
                                     John C. Maxwell

Looking back, I thought I was being a good husband and father.

I later understood that I used work as a place to hide.

Realizing all of this caused me deep pain. I remembered telling myself I was doing it for my family, for stability, for the future. The truth was simpler.

I was coping.

Choosing to heal meant I had to look again at a specific night at home that changed everything. A night so intense it lived behind my eyes for months. At the time, I did not want to deal with it, so I buried myself in motion. Meetings felt safer than feelings. Numbers were easier than grief. I called it leadership. It was survival.

If you are building a company to avoid what hurts, stop and look up. The cost is always paid by the people closest to you, including yourself. That is true whether you are single or partnered.

A single man can burn himself down in private. A partnered man burns a household without meaning to. Both are losses. The only starting point that works is self. Put healing first or the empire becomes a very expensive distraction.

I did not know that then. I was rewarded for being busy. The world handed me trophies for being away, for flying miles, for keeping the machine humming.

It is easy to confuse applause with alignment. It is easy to believe success means you are safe. I learned the opposite. The more accolades I gathered, the easier it became to ignore the voice that knew something was off.

I can see my origin story clearly now.

I grew up without much. I learned early that achievement could quiet the feeling that I was not enough. Voices from childhood told me I was never going to amount to anything.

I made a private promise to prove them wrong. That promise built careers. It also built a hole no achievement could fill. When my identity as a pastor collapsed, I replaced it with a new one as a businessman. The costume changed. The ache stayed the same.

After the collapse, I thought the shadow work was done. I had already faced my losses, felt the pain, and peeled away layers that held me back, or so I thought.

Then an amazing friend, we will call him "the Wizard" entered my life.

He was calm, grounded, and carried an understanding that I could not ignore. He introduced me to real shadow work, the kind that forced me to look beyond my excuses and directly into the mirror.

He asked me to sit in a chair and talk to my six-year-old self. Then he made me switch chairs and speak back to myself as that little boy, responding with raw truth.

At first it felt ridiculous, but as I sat there looking at that empty chair, tears came that I did not know I was still holding. I saw the fear of not being enough, the shame of past failures, and the belief that love had to be earned through performance.

That conversation changed me. It broke the illusion that the shadow was my enemy. It was simply a younger version of me asking to be seen, longing to be heard.

That process opened the door to deeper healing. Around the same time, I reconnected with an old networking friend from years ago, Jeremie, who invited me to explore an organization called The Mankind Project.

At first, I laughed it off. The idea of a men's circle sounded like something out of a hokey self help brochure. But something in me knew it was time.

What I found there was brotherhood without performance. Men who had nothing to prove. Men who listened without fixing. Those Thursday nights became another mirror, showing me where I still hid behind leadership titles instead of showing my humanity.

That work and circle gave me back something I didn't know I had lost.

Since then, everything has become a mirror. Every conflict, a signal. The shadow still whispers, but now it speaks truth instead of fear. It reminds me to stay honest with myself first, because the energy I bring into a room determines everything that follows.

The story ends here, but the lessons continue.

What follows isn't a recounting of events. It's what the fire revealed about leadership, energy, and the discipline of staying aligned when everything else falls away.

Energy Is the Real Strategy

Your nervous system is your brand. People feel you before they hear you.
You can dress it up with slides, data, and talking points, but if your energy is chaotic, everyone in the room feels it.

When your nervous system is dysregulated, your team mirrors it. A leader's shadow spreads faster than any memo.

Facing the shadow does not mean eliminating it. It means integrating it. When you name the fear, when you admit the insecurity, when you acknowledge the anger, it loses the power to silently steer. Shadows grow in silence. They shrink in honesty.

Leadership transformed by energy begins with self-honesty. The shadow will haunt every boardroom you enter until you decide to face it. But once you do, something powerful happens: the very shadow that haunted you becomes the reminder that alignment matters more than appearance.

Energy always tells the truth.

CEO POWER MOVES

REFLECT ON THIS CHAPTER

→ Leadership is energetic before it is strategic.
→ Shadows act as weights — they hold leaders down unless acknowledged.
→ Anchors ground you; weights drain you. Learn the difference.
→ Your nervous system is your brand. People feel your state before they hear your words.
→ Shadows grow in silence; they shrink in honesty.
→ Integration, not avoidance, is the path to authentic power.

What is relevant to you now?

_____

_____

_____

STOP LYING TO YOURSELF.
GET REAL. WRITE IT DOWN.

What shadows do you still have that you are aware of?

_____

_____

_____

How does your energy shift when you face conflict or criticism?

_____

_____

Where are you performing leadership instead of embodying it?

_____

_____

_____

_____

What part of you still believes you have to earn worthiness?

_____

_____

_____

Who do you trust to be completely honest with you that could help you mirror back what you cannot yet see?

_____

_____

_____

Who sees you as a leader and what would they say about you?

_____

_____

_____

_____

_____

_____

ANCHOR - CREATE A NEW HABIT

★ Begin each meeting with a few deep breaths to regulate your state.

★ When frustration appears, name the emotion out loud before it owns the room.

★ Replace "fixing" with listening — it transforms energy instantly.

★ End the week by asking, What shadow did I see, and what truth did it show me?

Integration is leadership. The shadow never fully leaves; it simply learns to walk beside you in the light.

Christopher Amato

CHAPTER 9

Leadership Transformed By Energy

"True leadership stems from individuality that is honestly and sometimes imperfectly expressed."
Sheryl Sandberg, COO of Meta

Rebuilding isn't about structure, it's about state.

Leadership begins with the energy you bring to it.

Every leader wants influence. Most think it comes from strategy, charisma, or authority, but real influence comes from energy.

Energy is the currency of leadership. Like any currency, it can be invested wisely or wasted carelessly.

For years, I spent energy like it was limitless. I chased validation, said yes to everything, poured myself into fixing problems that were not mine to fix. That is not investment, it is junk spending. Cheap withdrawals with nothing to show for them but exhaustion.

I got clear on two things:

> ***If your attention belongs to everyone else, you no longer belong to yourself.***

Being abundant doesn't mean dumping resources, it is about creating a flow of giving and receiving with good balance.

I also discovered the law of focused energy:

> ***Focused energy builds rhythm.***
> ***Rhythm builds momentum.***
> ***Momentum builds mastery.***

Mastery compounds into influence. This is not abstract. It is practical. The ROI of saying no is real. Every yes has a cost. Every no protects your future self.

Boundaries are not barriers. They are investments. Every time you close a leak, you multiply the energy available for what actually matters. Strong boundaries create respect. Weak boundaries invite disrespect.

The moment I stopped bleeding energy through over-explaining, guilt, or validation-chasing, I discovered an exponential truth: energy without leaks is unstoppable.

Start with what you can actually control:

Your 3-Ms

Mouth (the stories you speak),

Mind (the thoughts you feed),

Mood (the state you bring into the room).

Practices That Rebuilt Me

After shadow work, therapy, and finally sitting still long enough to feel peace again, I started rebuilding, not the company, but myself.

Mornings became sacred. Before touching my phone or checking email, I would do intentional breathwork, or pray, or sometimes just sit in silence until the storm inside me settled.

It was uncomfortable at first. My mind wanted to run. My body wanted to move.

Stillness felt like a threat.

Each morning, the silence stretched a little longer until it started to feel like power instead of punishment.

I began to write again, not reports or projections, but reflections. Small truths like, "Energy spent in fear has no return," or "Peace is the real profit." I wrote them on yellow pads and taped them above my desk until the reminders became reflex.

Slowly, the clutter cleared: in my mind, in my home, in my business ideas.

I noticed something profound.

When my energy was clean, opportunity flowed in without effort.

Calls came. Deals opened. Conversations felt natural again. It was as if the universe had been waiting for me to stop pushing long enough to receive.

Leadership no longer felt like pressure. It felt like stewardship, and a sacred responsibility to manage my energy.

That discipline changed everything.

My mornings became my strategy sessions with Source. My breath became my boardroom. And every day I showed up grounded, the people around me did too.

Energy as the New Strategy

Leadership transformed by energy is leadership aligned. Alignment creates acceleration.

Misaligned leaders are like cars driving with the emergency brake on: noisy, strained, and inefficient.

Aligned leaders move with clarity and speed.

Clarity beats complexity.

Complexity slows motion, scatters focus, and repels people.

Clarity attracts. Simplicity scales. The simplest plan, executed with focused energy, beats the most sophisticated strategy fueled by chaos.

Energy stewardship is leadership stewardship. Guard your energy like treasure. Invest it like capital, and direct it.

Strategy can be delegated.
Tasks can be delegated.
Energy cannot.

Your state is your responsibility!

When energy and strategy align, leadership becomes transformational, not because you pushed harder, but because you became a living signal of alignment.
People do not follow slides or slogans. They follow energy.

The same energy that rebuilds a life can rebuild an organization. The next stage is about applying that alignment to every decision, team, and system you touch.

CEO POWER MOVES

REFLECT ON THIS CHAPTER

→ Energy is the true currency of leadership. Invest it wisely.
→ Focused energy → rhythm → momentum → mastery.
→ Boundaries multiply energy by closing leaks.
→ Alignment creates acceleration; misalignment drags everything.
→ Clarity attracts; complexity repels.
→ Strategy and tasks can be delegated, but your energy never can.

What is relevant to you now?

_____

_____

_____

STOP LYING TO YOURSELF.

GET REAL. WRITE IT DOWN.

What story, thought, or mood (3M) leaks the most energy each day?

_____

_____

_____

What boundary could close your biggest energy leak this week?

_____

_____

_____

How can you begin to check your state before you lead?

_____

_____

_____

Recall a time you were sure you were right and were completely wrong. How you handle that memory reveals your maturity.

_____

_____

_____

What qualities in others most irritate you? Write them all down.

_____

_____

_____

_____

_____

How are you acting out these same traits, or behaviors?

_____

_____

_____

ANCHOR - CREATE A NEW HABIT

★ Begin each day with five deliberate breaths before checking notifications.

★ Write one truth each morning that aligns your energy before your strategy.

★ Protect your first hour — no meetings, no noise, only intention.

★ End the week by asking, Did my energy lead or follow this week?

Leadership is not about controlling outcomes. It is about becoming a channel clear enough for alignment to flow through you.

Christopher Amato

PART FOUR

THE SOUL OF LEADERSHIP

PART FOUR

THE SOUL OF LEADERSHIP

CHAPTER 10

Rising From The Ashes

"Adversity causes some men to break; others to break records."

William Arthur Ward

T here's a point where you have to get honest and rebuild.

For me, that turning point came when I began a 12-week transformation program with Andrea and Jeremie King. It was the first time I wasn't trying to fix the business.

I was finally willing to look at myself.

I came into that program burned out, frustrated, and carrying the weight of every past failure like it was welded to my identity. I didn't realize how much of my leadership had been driven by fear, pride, overwhelm, and the belief that I had to do everything alone.

My patterns were running me, not the other way around.

Over those twelve weeks, something shifted. Not all at once, and not in some dramatic movie-moment. It happened in honest conversations, uncomfortable realizations, and a slow return to the version of myself I thought I had lost.

I learned how my nervous system was affecting every decision I made. I learned why I was always stuck in "fix it" or "trying" mode, always bracing for impact. I saw how often I sacrificed myself in the name of being the responsible one.

I finally understood that true leadership isn't about holding up the world. It's about being aligned with the world inside you.

The work wasn't easy. It asked me to confront old stories, outdated survival strategies, and parts of myself I had buried beneath years of pushing and performing. Yet it also showed me how much power and clarity I still had underneath the rubble.

Those twelve weeks didn't just give me tools. They gave me back to myself, better.

This book exists because of that transformation. It exists because I stopped trying to outrun my past and learned to rewrite it. It exists because I allowed them to hold up a mirror and say what I needed to hear, "You're not broken. You're just ready to evolve."

If you're reading this and you feel the weight of burnout, confusion, or disconnection, know this: change is possible.

You are not too far gone.

You are not stuck.

You are simply one decision away from a completely different trajectory — the same way I was.

Christopher Amato

To learn more about the work that helped me rebuild my life and leadership, visit: andreaandjeremieking.com

What Changed in Me: The Four Shifts That Rebuilt My Leadership

Those twelve weeks revealed more than I can explain here, and four internal shifts changed me the most:

1. False Humility → Authentic Confidence

For years, I wore a version of humility that wasn't real. It looked like modesty, but it was actually fear of being judged, misunderstood, or seen as arrogant.

Through this work, I learned the difference between shrinking and true humility.
True humility is quiet confidence.

It doesn't apologize for existing.
It doesn't seek approval. It simply stands.

When I stopped hiding behind false humility, my presence strengthened, my communication sharpened, and people responded to me differently because I finally responded to myself differently.

2. Outsourcing Worth → Belonging to Myself

I spent most of my life trying to earn belonging in business, in relationships, and in every room I walked into.

What I didn't realize was that I was handing my value to everyone but me.

The shift was simple but life-changing:
Belonging doesn't come from other people.
It starts internally.
It's something you stop chasing and start claiming.

Once I understood that, I no longer needed the world to validate me.
I started leading from grounded self-worth instead of emptiness and overcompensation.

3. Old Wounds → Forgiveness as Release

Forgiveness used to feel like letting someone off the hook.
I resisted it because I thought it meant agreeing with what happened.

What I learned is that forgiveness isn't about the other person at all.
It's about releasing the weight that keeps you from moving.

When I began forgiving the people who shaped me, the situations that hardened me, and even my younger self, something opened.

My nervous system softened. My clarity sharpened.
The anger I carried for years finally had somewhere to go.

Forgiveness didn't make me weaker, it made me free.

4. Chaotic Hustle → Aligned Energy Use

Before the 12 week immersion, my default was to push harder, move faster, force outcomes, and then burn out trying to hold everything together.

I learned that leadership isn't built on speed.

It's built on alignment.

Understanding my own energetic patterns changed everything.

When I stopped treating urgency as a strategy, my decisions got clearer.
My actions got cleaner.
My results multiplied without the chaos.

The Result

These four shifts didn't give me a new identity, they stripped away everything that wasn't really me. They rebuilt the foundation I now lead from.

Grounded. Clear. Aligned.

When that changed, so did everything around me.

Opportunities returned, not through force, but through alignment. The people showing up in my world reflected the energy I had finally learned to hold: steady, grounded, open.

I used to think legacy was wealth and reach.

Today, legacy looks like subtraction. Subtract what drains my energy. Guard what restores it. Lead with clarity.

Choose the life that chooses me back.

The universe will keep bringing mirrors until we learn the lesson. Those mirrors are not punishments. They are invitations. Every one of them brought me closer to the man writing these words.

If this book is anything, let it be an interruption. Let it arrive earlier than my lessons arrived for me. If you recognize yourself in these pages, pause.

Ask what hurts. Ask what you are using work to avoid. Ask what would change if you loved yourself enough to stop performing. Write it down. Record yourself. Get REAL.

Healing is possible. Peace is possible. The same is true for business.

That's what this story has always been about. Not failure. Not success. Integration.

The collapse gave me humility. The healing gave me depth. The rebuilding gave me a choice.

I don't measure success by revenue anymore. I measure it by peace. And by that standard, I'm finally wealthier than I have ever been.

Collapse is not the end, it is the clearing.

Happiness comes and goes. Peace stays. I stopped chasing happiness and started protecting peace.

When everything fell apart, I thought I had failed. The empire crumbled. The masks cracked. The energy leaks caught up with me. Rising does not happen by addition. It happens by subtraction.

I had to strip away the noise, the clutter, the distractions that kept me pretending I was in control.

The ROI of saying no became my salvation.
Every "no" closed a leak. Every "no" created space. Every "no" made room for alignment.

Clarity appeared. Calm became my command.

A regulated nervous system does not just protect your health; it commands presence.

People feel alignment before they see it. Calm became louder than chaos. Success is not about being the most qualified. It is about being the most aligned.

Alignment creates acceleration. Misalignment drags you under. Alignment is what pulled me out of the ashes.

The Lesson in the Fire

It was in letting go and trusting that life was not against me but for me that I found my footing again.
The river I once feared would drown me became the current that carried me.

Time or alignment? That is the real question.

When you stop forcing, life delivers exactly what is meant for you in timing that is perfect.

The right people. The right connections. The right resources.
They all arrive when you stop chasing and start trusting.

The Phoenix does not rise by clinging to what burned down, it rises by surrendering to the fire, letting it consume what cannot last, and lifting from the ashes with wings stronger than before.

Stop Chasing Butterflies

Your life is a garden. Choose to plant responsibly. Plant that which is in alignment with your true self. Focus on it with positive energy. The "butterflies" will be attracted to what you have planted. What's meant for you lands where alignment lives. Stop chasing... radiate and ATTRACT!

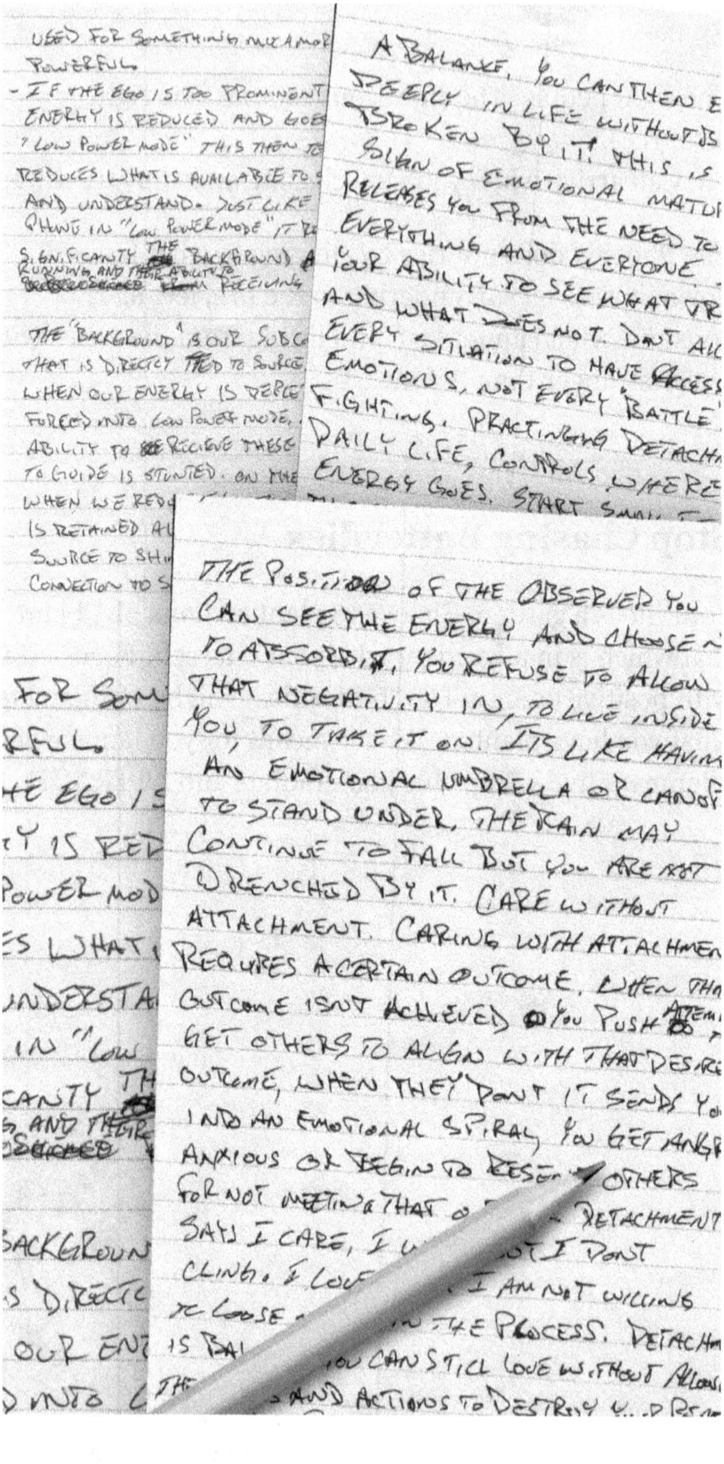

[Page 1 — top left, partially visible]

USED FOR SOMETHING MUCH MORE
POWERFUL.
- IF THE EGO IS TOO PROMINENT
ENERGY IS REDUCED AND GOES
"LOW POWER MODE" THIS THEN
REDUCES WHAT IS AVAILABLE TO
AND UNDERSTAND. JUST LIKE
PHONE IN "LOW POWER MODE" IT R
SIGNIFICANTLY THE BACKGROUND A
RUNNING AND THEIR ABILITY TO
~~PROCESSES FROM FEELING~~

THE "BACKGROUND" IS OUR SUBC
THAT IS DIRECTLY ~~TIED~~ TO SOURCE,
WHEN OUR ENERGY IS DEPLE
FORCED INTO LOW POWER MODE,
ABILITY TO ~~BE~~ RECIEVE THESE
TO GUIDE IS STUNTED. ON THE
WHEN WE RED
IS RETAINED A
SOURCE TO SH
CONNECTION TO S

FOR SOM
RFUL
HE EGO IS
TY IS RED
POWER MOD
ES WHAT
UNDERSTA
IN "LOW
CANTLY TH
S AND THEIR
~~SSSES~~

BACKGROUN
S DIRECTL
OUR EN IS BAL
INTO L TH

[Page 2 — top right]

A BALANCE. YOU CAN THEN E
DEEPLY IN LIFE WITHOUT B
BROKEN BY IT. THIS IS
SIGN OF EMOTIONAL MATUR
RELEASES YOU FROM THE NEED TO
EVERYTHING AND EVERYONE.
YOUR ABILITY TO SEE WHAT VR
AND WHAT DOES NOT. DON'T AL
EVERY SITUATION TO HAVE ACCESS
EMOTIONS. NOT EVERY BATTLE
FIGHTING. PRACTICING DETACHM
DAILY LIFE, CONTROLS WHERE
ENERGY GOES. START SMALL

[Page 3 — bottom / foreground]

THE POSITION OF THE OBSERVER YOU
CAN SEE THE ENERGY AND CHOOSE N
TO ABSORB IT. YOU REFUSE TO ALLOW
THAT NEGATIVITY IN, TO LIVE INSIDE
YOU, TO TAKE IT ON. ITS LIKE HAVING
AN EMOTIONAL UMBRELLA OR CANOP
TO STAND UNDER. THE RAIN MAY
CONTINUE TO FALL BUT YOU ARE NOT
DRENCHED BY IT. CARE WITHOUT
ATTACHMENT. CARING WITH ATTACHMEN
REQUIRES A CERTAIN OUTCOME. WHEN THA
OUTCOME ISN'T ACHIEVED ~~AS YOU PUSH B~~ ATTEM
GET OTHERS TO ALIGN WITH THAT DESIRE
OUTCOME, WHEN THEY DON'T IT SENDS Y
INTO AN EMOTIONAL SPIRAL. YOU GET ANGR
ANXIOUS OR BEGIN TO RESENT OTHERS
FOR NOT MEETING THAT O   DETACHMENT
SAYS I CARE, I U   T I DON'T
CLING, I LOVE
                    I AM NOT WILLING
TO LOOSE   IN THE PROCESS. DETACHM
               YOU CAN STILL LOVE WITHOUT ALLOW
         AND ACTIONS TO DESTROY U... DRE

CEO POWER MOVES

REFLECT ON THIS CHAPTER

→ Collapse is not the end; it is the preparation for rebirth.
→ Subtraction creates space for clarity and alignment.
→ The state of calm is that of command. A regulated nervous system changes everything.
→ Success comes from alignment, not qualification.
→ Don't chase, attract.
→ The Phoenix does not rebuild the ashes, it rises from them.

What is relevant to you now?

_____

_____

_____

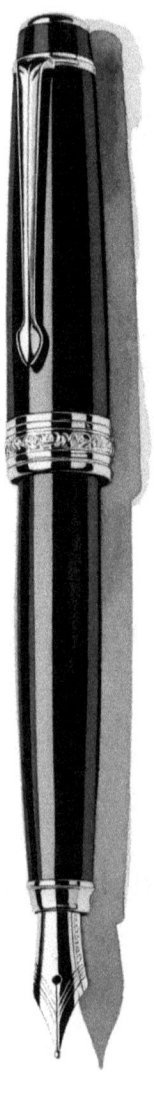

STOP LYING TO YOURSELF. GET REAL. WRITE IT DOWN.

What burned away that you are still trying to rebuild?

_____

_____

_____

How can you model regulation for those who mirror your energy?

_____

_____

_____

How would calm leadership change the energy of your home or business?

_____

_____

_____

In what areas are you chasing opportunity (butterflies), or creating space (a garden) for it to arrive?

_____

_____

_____

_____

_____

_____

What does your own Phoenix moment look like in motion?

_____

_____

_____

_____

_____

_____

_____

_____

_____

ANCHOR - CREATE A NEW HABIT

★ Subtract one distraction that drains your clarity.

★ When urgency rises, slow your breath before you act.

★ Replace one act of forcing with one act of trust.

★ End each day by naming one way life supported you today.

Rising is not about rebuilding what was lost. It is about becoming the kind of leader who no longer needs the old empire to feel whole.

Christopher Amato

CHAPTER 11

The CEO As An Example Of Healing

"If your actions inspire others to dream more, learn more, do more and become more, you are a leader."

John C. Maxwell

When I stopped chasing, life started delivering.

Not all at once, but consistently.

Like a sunrise instead of lightning. Opportunities returned, but this time they matched my peace. I started consulting again, but from alignment, not desperation.

The deals came to me instead of being forced into existence. My phone stopped feeling like an alarm clock and started feeling like a tool for purpose.

Then, love showed up. After the storm of heartbreak, I met someone who mirrored the calm I had spent years building within myself. It was unfamiliar, yet easy, honest, steady.

For the first time, I was not trying to prove my worth. I was simply living it. That relationship became evidence of everything I had learned: you do not attract what you want; you attract what you are.

It feels different because I am different. We talk openly about everything, the way change can unsettle a home, the fear that old patterns might return.

I share my anxiety rather than hide it. She shares her needs rather than guessing about mine. Partnership means holding space for each other to become. It also means knowing when to get quiet and trust the flow. Control kept me safe once. Surrender keeps me honest now.

Around the same time, my business life evolved. Partnerships formed with a clarity I had never experienced before.

Conversations were grounded.

Negotiations felt natural.

I was no longer the man fighting for survival; I was the man teaching others how to rebuild from truth.

Coaching became less about systems and more about energy and helping others find alignment the way I had.

The Phoenix moment wasn't a single breakthrough. It was the daily practice of staying aligned, of trusting the process, of letting life meet me halfway.

Looking back, every loss was a lesson. Every descent was data. Every collapse was the foundation for clarity. The fire never destroyed me. It refined me.

What if the real measure of a leader was healing?

For too long, leadership has been defined by power, profit, and performance.

Leadership starts inside.

You cannot lead others if you cannot lead yourself. Self-control creates external control. Inner chaos always becomes outer chaos.

A CEO who refuses to face their pain will unconsciously spread that pain into every area of life.

A CEO who chooses healing creates a ripple effect that reaches far beyond the boardroom.

Energy is identity. Who you are is how you show up.
I have said it before, but it bears repeating:

> **You do not attract what you want. You attract what you are.**

People may listen to your words, but they will always follow your energy. A dysregulated nervous system signals weakness no matter how confident the language.

A regulated nervous system signals conviction no matter how soft the words. Calm is the command.

From Noise to Light

The noise of ego is what blinds us.
If you have ever stepped away from the city lights and looked at the night sky, you know the brilliance that appears when the noise goes dark.

What noise can you switch off so your real brilliance can appear?
Leaders who dull their ego, stop performing and start listening, reveal something greater: Source.

Light only comes from Source. When a leader opens themselves to it, the entire organization transforms.

Because the soul of a CEO is not measured in deals closed or titles earned.
It is measured in the lives they impact by the example they set. The deals, titles and money come, more as a byproduct when leading from a healed place.

Healing does not make you less of a CEO.
It makes you more of one.

Christopher Amato

CEO POWER MOVES

REFLECT ON THIS CHAPTER

→ Leadership starts inside: self-control creates external control.
→ Energy is identity. You attract what you are.
→ Calm is the command; regulation signals real strength.
→ Ego creates light noise; reduce it to reveal Source.
→ A healing CEO transforms organizations through presence, not performance.
→ Authenticity builds trust faster than authority ever could.

What is relevant to you now?

_____

_____

_____

_____

STOP LYING TO YOURSELF. GET REAL. WRITE IT DOWN.

Where does your ego still turn up the volume?

_____

_____

How do people feel after leaving your presence — calmer or more tense?

_____

_____

What would change if healing, not hustle, became your leadership metric?

_____

_____

_____

_____

_____

How can you model regulation for those who mirror your energy?

_____

_____

_____

_____

_____

What artificial "light" are other people bringing that is interrupting your true light, and how can you create better boundaries with them?

_____

_____

_____

_____

How can you see this as self care?

_____

_____

_____

ANCHOR - CREATE A NEW HABIT

★ Begin each meeting with a shared breath to ground the room. (If you haven't noticed by now, intentional breath work is a huge key!)

★ Replace one performance habit with a moment of genuine connection.

★ When ego noise rises, pause and remember: Light only comes from Source.

★ End each day by asking, Did my energy heal or harm today?

The soul of leadership is not control, it's consciousness. When you heal, you do not just change yourself, you change what leadership means for everyone watching.

Christopher Amato

CHAPTER 12

Legacy Beyond Wealth

"A leader's legacy is only as strong as the foundation they leave behind that allows others to continue to advance the organization in their name. Legacy is not the memory of better times when the old leader was there. That's not legacy, that's nostalgia."

Simon Sinek

I used to believe leadership meant keeping the mask on.

Steady voice, straight posture, and no cracks. Then one day, I watched a man struggle through something personal and instinctively wanted to offer the same empty reassurances I had been given for years.

I stopped before my mouth opened and saw myself in him — the burnout, the pride, the quiet panic of pretending it was all fine. Instead of offering advice, I told the truth. "I know what that feels like. I've been there."

At that moment, something shifted. The conversation changed from performance to presence. He exhaled. I did too. The air in the room softened. I realized that the greatest power a leader has is not authority; it's authenticity.

Every time I showed up real, the people around me showed up real too. Every time I regulated before I reacted, the energy in the room changed before a single word was spoken.

These days, I lead differently. Meetings start with a breath. Conversations start with curiosity, not defense. I still demand excellence, but I pair it with empathy. Collaborations move faster not because of pressure, but because of trust.

Clients sense it. Partners sense it.

Healing made me quieter, but also stronger.

Calm became the loudest voice in the room.

Wealth is measurable. Legacy is not.

For years, I thought the point of accumulating revenue, recognition, and respect would fulfill me. Wealth fades. Markets shift. Titles get forgotten.

What outlives you is not what you owned, it's what you embodied.

Legacy begins with alignment. Misalignment drains more than money; it drains people, culture, and trust. Alignment produces compound returns, not just in business but in lives.
 The leader who embodies alignment doesn't just create profits; they create conviction. And conviction spreads far beyond balance sheets.

The Shift from Accumulation to Alignment

When the dust finally settled, I sat in my office surrounded by symbols.

Things I used to think meant I was a success: awards, contracts, framed photos from company galas.

They didn't move me anymore.

These days, the mirror matters more than the trophy case.

What meant something were the handwritten notes from employees whose lives had changed because I finally learned how to lead with heart.

The call from a client telling me that our conversation helped him fix his marriage. Those were priceless reflections of who I had become, and priceless in a way my P&L could never capture.

I started mentoring a few men who reminded me of myself ten years earlier — driven, brilliant, unknowingly broken. Watching them wake up to their own patterns became one of the most fulfilling experiences of my life.

I didn't have to teach them strategy.

They already knew how to win. What they needed was permission to stop performing and start healing. That became my legacy: not the deals I closed, but the men I helped guide to their inner truth, their own personal healing.

Now, when I look at wealth, I see it differently.

Money is energy — a tool, not an identity. It amplifies who you are. If you're aligned, wealth becomes fuel for impact. If you're unhealed, it becomes gasoline for chaos.

My job now is to ensure what I pass down, in business, in family, and in community, carries alignment with it.

Legacy without soul is just inheritance. Legacy with soul becomes light.

Self-trust is the highest currency. Without it, you'll always chase validation. With it, you create confidence that anchors teams, families, and communities. Conviction commands.

When you know who you are and what you stand for, people align to it.

They remember it. That becomes your legacy.

Too many leaders build wealth and leave wounds. They pass down assets but no wisdom. Businesses but no soul. The next generation inherits the mess their success was built on.

The leaders who heal, who prioritize alignment over accumulation, pass down something greater: a blueprint for how to live whole.

Is your wealth an anchor or a weight? Wealth can be an anchor, grounding future generations, or it can be a weight, crushing them with pressure.

Christopher Amato

The difference is whether it's rooted in healing.

Legacy without soul becomes burden. Legacy with soul becomes blessing.

When my empire crumbled, I thought I had lost everything. But in the ashes, I found clarity: wealth may provide comfort, but legacy provides meaning.

Legacy beyond wealth is the only legacy that lasts.

Epilogue – The Quiet Legacy

There is a moment when the noise fades and you finally hear yourself breathe.

The numbers, the headlines, and the expectations all quiet down. In that silence, you meet the one person you've been chasing your entire life: yourself.

You see the man who built empires and the one who burned them down. You see the boy who tried to prove his worth and the soul who finally understood he already had it.

You stop running.

You stop performing.

You stop needing the world to clap for you, and in that stillness, something shifts.

The hunger turns into peace. The striving becomes gratitude. Legacy stops being about what people remember you for and starts being about how deeply you lived while you were here.

That's the moment I knew I was free. The story ends here, but the work continues.

Healing is not a finish line — it's a practice. Leadership is not a title — it's a frequency.

Everyone who reads these words stands at a threshold. The fall, the rebuild, and the rise all exist within you, too.

Your empire may look different, but the pattern is the same.

This is not the story of my success; it's the story of remembrance: coming home to truth, to peace, to self.

The next pages are not lessons from a teacher. They are echoes from experience. A compass, not a map.

The soul of a CEO is not measured by numbers. It's revealed by integrity, by embodiment, by the ripple effect of a healed man leading with truth.

Christopher Amato

CEO POWER MOVES

REFLECT ON THIS CHAPTER

- → Wealth fades; legacy endures.
- → Legacy begins with alignment, not accumulation.
- → Self-trust is the highest currency; conviction commands.
- → Too many leaders pass down assets but not wisdom; healing creates true inheritance.
- → Legacy without soul becomes burden; legacy with soul becomes blessing.
- → Money amplifies who you already are. Heal first, then build.

What is relevant to you now?

_____

_____

_____

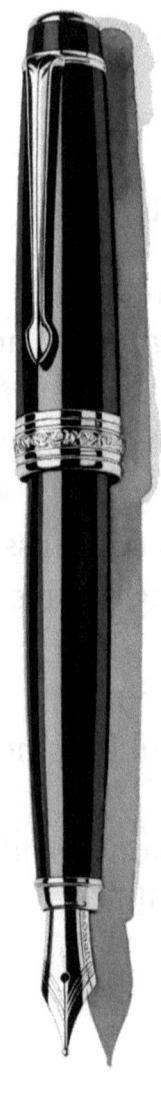

STOP LYING TO YOURSELF.
GET REAL. WRITE IT DOWN.

What kind of inheritance are you building — assets or alignment?

_____

_____

_____

How would your business look if it reflected your healed self, not your survival self?

_____

_____

_____

Where are you still chasing validation disguised as ambition?

_____

_____

_____

What have you accomplished that you are proud of?

_____

_____

_____

_____

_____

_____

_____

What will people remember about your energy, not your accolades or achievements?

_____

_____

_____

Who are you mentoring right now that could carry your light forward?

_____

_____

ANCHOR - CREATE A NEW HABIT

★ Audit what you're building — how much of it is for ego, and how much is for impact?

★ Share one truth from your healing journey with someone who needs it.

★ Replace one "legacy purchase" with a "legacy conversation."

★ End the week by asking: Did I build from alignment today, or accumulation?

Legacy is not what you leave behind. It's what you leave within. The soul of a CEO is not the story of what he built. It's the story of who he became.

Preface to the CEO Manifesto

The following are not rules. They are reminders.

Reminders that:

- Leadership begins in the body.
- Alignment is power.
- Calm is command.

This Manifesto is not about building an empire.
It's about:

- Leading an empire from your heart and soul.
- Remembering that energy leads before language.
- Trusting that peace is presence, and that no strategy outperforms self-awareness.

Use this version, or write your own and review it daily.

Manifesto: The Soul Of A CEO

I am no longer impressed by busy work.
I am no longer fooled by balance sheets that shine while souls collapse.
I am no longer seduced by the illusion that success without soul is victory.

I believe leadership is energetic before it is strategic.
I believe energy is identity, and I attract what I am, not what I wish for.
I believe clarity is command, and calm is power.

I reject the false gods of productivity, validation, and control.
I reject the myth that more is always better.
I reject the lie that leadership requires self-betrayal.

I choose alignment over accumulation.
I choose discipline over distraction.
I choose subtraction over noise.

I choose to lead from a nervous system that is calm, a soul that is whole, and a conviction that is unshakable.

I am defined by presence. By healing. By the energy I steward and the legacy I leave.

This is the way forward. This is the rebirth.
This is the soul of a CEO.

A Letter to My 30ish Self

Hey Chris,

You're ambitious. You're hungry. You see the path in front of you and you're ready to sprint down it. I admire that about you. That fire built everything we are in 2025.

There's something I need you to hear before you take off.

Take care of yourself. Take this seriously.

You think you're supposed to hold everything together by force. You think being tired is normal, and running on empty is a requirement of success. You think sacrificing yourself is the price of entry.

It isn't.

Your energy is going to become the most valuable currency you have. It will determine how you lead, who you attract, and how far you go. If you don't protect it, everything you're building will eventually feel heavier than it should.

I'm telling you this now because I wish someone had told us then: Love yourself like you matter because you do.

Fill your own cup every single day. Not once in a while, not when things fall apart, not when you finally have time. Every day. Even if it's five minutes. Even if it feels selfish. Even if you don't understand why it matters yet.

You're going to carry teams, companies, and people.

You will build things that outlive your mistakes. You will do work that comes from the deepest part of you. And when you're steady on the inside, you'll lead with clarity that people can feel.

Strength won't come from grinding harder.
Strength will come from treating your mind, body, and heart like the primary assets of the business.

Eat well. Rest without guilt. Move your body. Slow down before you collapse. Choose people who support the man you're becoming. Breathe and clear the noise. Don't apologize for needing space. Don't minimize what you feel. Don't wait for pain to make you pay attention.

You don't earn your worth by overextending yourself. You earn it by showing up whole.

If you take anything from this letter, take this:
The business will grow. The opportunities will come. The wins will stack. And the future version of you (me) — will have the life you're working so hard for.

You are allowed to care about you, and be human. When you take care of yourself, everything else gets easier. I'm here because you kept going.

With respect,
Christopher 2025

Christopher Amato

ABOUT THE AUTHOR

Christopher Amato is an award-winning CEO, entrepreneur, and leader with a lifelong commitment to service, growth, and transformation. Known for his passion for people and community, he has spent decades helping others rebuild their lives in business and beyond it.

He is a two-time CEO of the Year recipient from California business publications and has negotiated more than $100 million in contracts while raising tens of millions in capital across multiple industries.

For twelve years, Christopher worked directly with at-risk and underprivileged youth in California and Arizona, developing programs focused on addiction recovery, depression support, and suicide prevention. That work continues to shape his approach to leadership — one that balances profit with purpose and strategy with soul.

He holds a Bachelor's degree in Finance and an MBA in Business Management. Over more than three decades as a serial entrepreneur, he has owned and operated nine companies, scaling teams, systems, and operations with a consistent focus on sustainable growth.

One of those ventures, an FDA-licensed over-the-counter drug manufacturing facility, earned him the International Exporter of the Year Award from the U.S. Small Business Administration for increasing export business by 300 percent in a single year.

Today, Christopher channels his experience into helping leaders find alignment, clarity, and conviction, transforming the way business is built from the inside out. His dedication to empowering others, combined with a proven track record of results with integrity, makes him a powerful example of leadership with soul.

Credits

Author:
Christopher Amato

Book Development & Production:
Junction 42 Studio - jct42.com - Andrea & Jeremie King

Developmental Editing, Manuscript Architecture, Interior Formatting, and Production Management by Andrea King. Cover Direction and Brand Alignment by Andrea & Jeremie King.

Publisher:
Amato International LLC

www.ingramcontent.com/pod-product-compliance
Lightning Source LLC
Chambersburg PA
CBHW050635160426
43194CB00010B/1680